"WE SERV

WAR-TIME
WANDSWORTH AND BATTERSEA
1939-1945

by Anthony Shaw and Jon Mills

Wandsworth Borough Council

"WE SERVED"

WAR-TIME
WANDSWORTH AND BATTERSEA
1939-1945

© Wandsworth Borough Council

Published by
Wandsworth Borough Council
Leisure and Amenity Services Department

Designed and produced by
Publicity and Print Section,
Wandsworth Borough Council
August 1989.

Printed by
Lundie Brothers Ltd., Croydon.

ISBN 0 902837 19 2

INTRODUCTION

Many residents of the present Borough of Wands-worth will not have been born until after the war, while others will have settled here since 1945. This book, which has been produced to commemorate the fiftieth anniversary of the start of World War Two in September 1939, aims to give an idea of what it was like to live through those times. It is not intended to enumerate every bomb that dropped but to tell of the people, their hardships, bravery, ingenuity, humour and doggedness, which saw them through that difficult period.

I would like to thank Jon Mills and Bob Jenner for providing essential material, without which the book would be incomplete. Also my thanks to all those who wrote to me with their reminiscences and supplied photographs, which give a personal touch to the story. If anybody has any further information or photographs, I would be glad to hear from them. Any details will be added to the files of the Local History Library at the Battersea Library, 265 Lavender Hill, London SWll lJB.

ANTHONY SHAW,
LOCAL HISTORY LIBRARIAN

MEN! YOU ARE WANTED

—TO FIGHT FIRE!

MEN OVER 25, and youths of 14–18, you are urgently wanted for London's Auxiliary Fire Service. The training is carried out at your local fire station; it is interesting and exciting. Training is given in the evenings or in the afternoons by members of the regular Fire Brigade. It need take up no more than a couple of hours a week, but you can, if you like, spend more time at it, and go out on calls with the 'regulars'. What *is* essential is that you join *now*. On you depends the safety of your family, of the women and children, in case of fire caused by raiding bombers. The regular Fire Brigade alone could not possibly cope with the widespread fires that an air raid would cause. Women are wanted also, as drivers, telephonists and clerks. The call is clear and urgent to every eligible man and woman who reads this. It's no good saying, 'A.R.P. will look after everything' A.R.P. is *you*! So go along to your local fire station to-day, or learn all about the Auxiliary Fire Service by posting the coupon below.

X marks the spot! You have to know your way about when fire breaks out. And these A.F.S. recruits seem to be finding their map reading most interesting.

All work and no play makes Jack a dull boy! Here you see a typical scene in an A.F.S. recreation room. According to the station you join, you can enjoy darts and other games in the best of company.

NOW IS THE BEST TIME TO JOIN! — POST THIS COUPON NOW!

To the Chief Officer, London Fire Brigade Headquarters, Albert Embankment, S.E.1.

Please *send me full particulars* of the A.F.S.

Name ....

Address ....

....

Post in ½d. unsealed envelope

ISSUED BY THE LONDON COUNTY COUNCIL

B.L.S. 10/3/3

PREPARATIONS

At 11am on September 3rd, 1939, the Prime Minister, Neville Chamberlain, broadcast on the wireless to the people of Great Britain to tell them that the country was at war with Germany. Two minutes later a sound was heard in the streets of Wandsworth and Battersea which was to become very familiar during the next six years, the wail of the air raid siren. On this first occasion it was a false alarm, caused by an unidentified civilian aeroplane approaching the English coast from France, but thanks to forethought by the Government and years of hard work by dedicated local volunteers the inhabitants of the two boroughs were ready for such an occurrence, and all the Air Raid Precautions (A.R.P.) services were at their war-stations. The start of actual aerial attacks in the boroughs was to be delayed for almost exactly a year but the system which existed on the day war broke out was to survive almost unaltered throughout the war.

In October 1935 the Home Office sent to the Councils of all the London Metropolitan Boroughs a circular suggesting measures which might be taken by the authorities to protect their populations against possible hostile attack from the air. Councils were urged to consider devising schemes for 'air-raid precautions' and were asked to send delegates to a conference to discuss the problem. The two boroughs responded very differently to the circular. Wandsworth decided immediately to send the Mayor, the Town Clerk, the Borough Engineer and the Medical Officer of Health as its representatives to the conference. Battersea's response was very different. The Council, firmly believing that there could be no defence against attacks from the air with high explosive bombs and poison gas, proposed the motion on 24th October that 'they cannot be expected to assume the responsibility or be saddled with the cost of matters outside their normal range of functions'. The motion was carried by 24 votes to nil. As an afterthought they added that their duties would be performed in time of war, out of common humanity.

Opposition to any form of air-raid precautions seems to have been fairly widespread in Battersea. At the same meeting in October, the councillors received a deputation of ratepayers and a letter from the Battersea Branch of the Amalgamated Society of Woodworkers, both declaring their opposition to any measure connected with A.R.P.

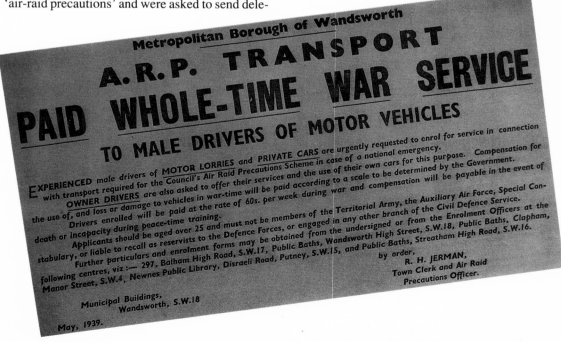

Metropolitan Borough of Wandsworth

A.R.P. TRANSPORT

PAID WHOLE-TIME WAR SERVICE

TO MALE DRIVERS OF MOTOR VEHICLES

EXPERIENCED male drivers of MOTOR LORRIES and PRIVATE CARS are urgently requested to enrol for service in connection with transport required for the Council's Air Raid Precautions Scheme in case of a national emergency. Compensation for the use of, and loss or damage to vehicles in war-time will be paid according to a scale to be determined by the Government.

OWNER DRIVERS are also asked to offer their services and the use of their own cars for this purpose. Compensation will be payable in the event of death or incapacity during peace-time training.

Drivers enrolled will be paid at the rate of 60s. per week during war and compensation will be payable in the event of

Applicants should be aged over 25 and must not be members of the Territorial Army, the Auxiliary Air Force, Special Constabulary, or liable to recall as reservists to the Defence Forces, or engaged in any other branch of the Civil Defence Service.

Further particulars and enrolment forms may be obtained from the undersigned or from the Enrolment Officers at the following centres, viz :— 297, Balham High Road, S.W.17, Public Baths, Wandsworth High Street, S.W.18, Public Baths, Clapham, Manor Street, S.W.4, Newnes Public Library, Disraeli Road, Putney, S.W.15, and Public Baths, Streatham High Road, S.W.16.

by order,

R. H. JERMAN,
Town Clerk and Air Raid
Precautions Officer.

Municipal Buildings,
Wandsworth, S.W.18

May, 1939.

MR. A.M. ROSS DISTRICT
WARDEN OF WANDSWORTH

The reluctance of Battersea to consider an A.R.P. scheme is understandable in the climate of the time. Military theorists had been predicting since the 1920s that in the next war knockout blows would be delivered to major cities such as London by vast air forces dropping poison gas, high-explosive and incendiary bombs. The idea grew up, even amongst experts, that nothing could stop the bomber aircraft of an enemy power from performing this destruction and that therefore any measures to survive such attacks would only serve to encourage an enemy rather than deter him. This attitude, combined with a reluctance to spend any locally-raised revenue on terms dictated by Central Government was to cause many problems for both Councils for the next few years.

As a result of their attendance at the Home Office Conference in October, and after the receipt of further guiding notes from the Government, the Council of Wandsworth instructed its officers in May 1936 to prepare a report on the measures which might be taken to give protection to the borough's population. By July a preliminary report had been submitted and the problems which it raised had been passed to the Home Office for advice. The Council had already realised that the work involved in devising a scheme of protection was very arduous and it was happy to accept the offer of full-time help from Councillor Capt. Paton Reid in July, 1936.

The problems which the committees were studying at this point were common to all local authorities. The two main weapons most likely to be used were poison gas and bombs. Authorities had to devise some means of preserving communications, provide services to decontaminate people and goods contaminated by poison gas, provide for the rescue and care of casualties and to provide training and recruitment for all the services needed to provide these measures.

By October 1936, the preliminary scheme for Wandsworth had been approved by the Home Office but in Battersea little had happened since the meeting of a year earlier. In that month the Council sent its Senior Sanitary Inspector to the Home Office Civilian Anti-Gas School in Gloucestershire, to learn of the dangers and techniques of this new sort of warfare and a separate Air Raid Precautions Committee was formed with representatives from all the Council committees who might be involved in A.R.P. serving on it. Three months later Wandsworth took its own skeleton scheme one stage further by advertising in the local press and on posters for volunteers to help with A.R.P.

For Wandsworth, 1937 was a year in which the Council began to make the public aware of the problems which they might have to face in war. It began with advertisements on posters and in the local papers asking for volunteers for the new A.R.P. services. Correspondence was conducted with the owners of many buildings in the borough to assess the suitability of various premises for use as First Aid Posts, Air-raid Shelters and Gas De-contamination Centres. In March it was suggested that an A.R.P. exhibition should be held in the Town Hall, to make more people aware of the services which were being provided in the borough. This exhibition was held from 25th June to 3rd July and was visited by over 5,000 people. Two thousand people attended the lectures given by the council's Anti-Gas Instructor at the exhibition. Although not designed to recruit for the A.R.P. services, it must still have been a disappointment to find only sixty-five new volunteers enrolling for service. As a result of this exhibition, a permanent A.R.P. Enquiry Bureau was set up in the Municipal Buildings for the enrolment of volunteers and the sale of A.R.P. publications.

In Battersea, 1937 was a year of slow improvement. A steady stream of council employees attended the Anti-Gas School and the Council loaned premises to both the Red Cross and the British Medical Association for a series of lectures on first aid. In March, the Council accepted the offer of help from the Home Office of a full-time A.R.P. adviser. Capt. C.J. Toyne commenced duty on 8th April but resigned seven months later to be replaced by Paymaster-Capt. A.C. Colles R.N. (Retd.). In the early part of the year, Battersea Borough Council was involved in a political squabble which was to frustrate its efforts at creating an efficient A.R.P. service. In common with many local authorities, and particularly those which were Labour controlled, Battersea felt that the cost of all expenditure on A.R.P. measures should be borne by Central Government. In April, the Metropolitan Boroughs Standing Committee passed a motion to that effect. Battersea concurred with the motion and proposed to defer consideration of all A.R.P. services involving substantial expenditure. It obviously felt, however, that £58 did not constitute a substantial sum as it approved expenditure of that amount on the conversion of the harness room at the Council's Falcon Wharf Depot into an A.R.P. lecture room.

1938 was to prove the turning point in the establishment of the A.R.P. services. The year was to see the implementation of an Air Raid Precautions Act which made it a statutory duty for local authorities to devise measures for safeguarding their populations from the effects of air raids. The Act cleared up the anomalies regarding expenditure on A.R.P., ruling that between 60% and 75% of approved expenditure would be recoverable from the Government. The Act also clarified which services the local authorities must provide and which would be provided by Central Government. In Wandsworth and Battersea the division of services was fairly clear cut. The London County Council was to be responsible for the provision of fire and ambulance services, the lighting and cleaning of main roads and for the recruiting and training of the required personnel. The local authorities, with advice and financial help from Central Government, were to be responsible for all other services. The A.R.P. scheme devised for Battersea and Wandsworth varied in detail but were broadly similar. Each system was based on Air Raid Wardens who were responsible for protective measures and advice in a particular street or area in their own locality. In the event of air-raid damage they would report, via the telephone, to a local control staff who would report back to a borough control centre. This control would call on further services for aid and co-ordinate the provision of all services to 'air-raid incidents'. On call were specialists like the Rescue Squads, who dealt with people trapped in collapsed buildings and demolished unsafe buildings. Decontamination Squads dealt with any contamination by poison gas. Although not under the direct control of the council, the control staff could mobilise the Fire and Ambulance Services, the Police and the public utility companies such as water, gas and electricity. If the services in the borough were overwhelmed, the controls would then call on assistance from other boroughs.

It is interesting to note that with only a few changes prompted by operational experience, and later a manpower shortage, this basic system was used throughout the war.

The passing of the Act and its provision for Government grants gave the more go-ahead authorities such as Wandsworth the chance to expand their services quickly. In March, six temporary enrolment officers were appointed to handle the steady flow of volunteers for the service. On the 14th March, the Secretary of State for Home Affairs broadcast an appeal for volunteers for A.R.P. and a leaflet available from Post Offices listed the services for which men and women could volunteer. The Council printed and distributed its own leaflet asking for volunteers and listing Council offices where advice was available. In May, approval was given for the erection of a purpose-built first aid and decontamination centre behind the Municipal Buildings in Shoreham Street at a cost of £5,800. In the same month the borough was chosen by the Home Office to take part in an experimental survey to estimate the air-raid shelter requirements of people who might be caught in the street by a daylight raid. The Metropolitan Police conducted a survey of the number of people in the main streets, whilst the Council looked at the basements of all nearby premises to assess the work needed to make them suitable as air-raid shelters. As a result of pressure from the Home Office, the Council also considered the problem of how to store enough gas masks for the population of the borough, which would be distributed in an emergency.

METROPOLITAN
BOROUGH OF BATTERSEA.

AIR RAID
WARDEN.

LOND
DEFE

THIS IS TO CERTIFY THAT
JOY, EDWARD FREDK. GEORGE
Full Name in BLOCK Letters.

National Registration Number

ABBK 166 1

has been appointed a *Post Invasion Warden*
in the Invasion Defence Organisation of
Battersea
Local Authority Area.

R.G.R....
Invasion Defence Officer.
29th October 1942

This slip must be surrendered to the Invasion Defence Officer on his demand or if the holder resigns, or leaves the area.

(C46622) 100,000 10/42

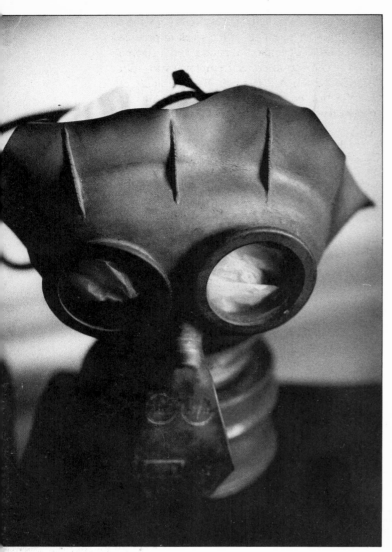

CHILD'S 'MICKEY MOUSE' GAS MASK

worth, the Council's depot at Ashlone Wharf, Putney and an upstairs room at Streatham Baths. They were also asked to accept consignments of sandbags and quantities of anti-gas clothing which were eventually stored in the Municipal Buildings, At a Council meeting at the end of July the A.R.P. Sub-Committee reported that to date 3,235 people had volunteered for A.R.P. work. Of those, 1,055 had been trained. Although well above strength for First Aid workers, the borough had only just over one third of the wardens required.

Since the A.R.P. Act of 1937 imposed a duty on local authorities to make provisions for their population, Battersea could not avoid some work on A.R.P. but progress was slow. In April 1938, they announced that the converted harness room at Falcon Wharf was to be used as a training centre for Air-raid wardens until the conversion of a special room over the Register Office at Southlands. Falcon Wharf was eventually to be used as a depot for the Rescue Service. In the same month the Council advertised for a full-time A.R.P. instructor and two full-time head wardens; the latter were both considered to be temporary posts. To encourage A.R.P.

BABY'S ANTI-GAS C

As the largest borough in London, Wandsworth had many problems in the organisation of its A.R.P. services. This was recognised in July by the creation of six decentralised 'divisional offices' for A.R.P., one in each of the five parliamentary constituencies of the borough, except for Balham and Tooting for which an office in each centre was provided. These offices were staffed by the enrolment officers appointed in March. Except for the Putney office which was located at the Newnes Public Library in Disraeli Road, all the offices were located in the Public Baths of the districts. By the end of July the borough had been provisionally divided into Wardens Sectors and work had begun on the allocation of wardens' reporting posts.

The heightening of international tension in the summer of 1938 prompted the Home Office to urge local authorities to take delivery of their allocations of A.R.P. stores as soon as possible. Wandsworth was told that by the end of August it should expect to receive 330,000 civilian gas masks. After failing to find accommodation for them in local schools, it was arranged that they should be divided between the public library at West Hill, Wands-

recruitment, all Council offices were kept open until 9pm on three nights of the week to provide information to potential volunteers and a special appeal was made to council employees to offer their services for A.R.P. work. By the middle of May the first course of instruction for Air-raid wardens had started at Falcon Wharf and a tempo-rary 'gas chamber' had been erected at Southlands to test the effectiveness of gas masks. Bowing to pressure from the Home Office to accept consign-ments of gas masks for the local people, the Council estimated in June that they would require five stores to hold the necessary 30,000 masks and accordingly placed advertisements in the papers asking for suitable space. In July, the Council's A.R.P. training centre at Southlands was finally completed and the first badges and proficiency cer-tificates were awarded to the volunteers, who at this date numbered 204.

By August 1938, both boroughs had made some advances with their A.R.P. preparations. Wandsworth, with its larger area, more affluent population and traditions of voluntary work, had advanced its preparations further than had Bat-tersea. Both authorities probably felt that the work they were doing would never be required. Events in September were not only to awaken everyone to the real possibility of war, but also to initiate measures that would stand them in good stead when war was declared just over one year later.

BATTERSEA WARDENS AT
'SOUTHLANDS' 1940

1939

In 1939, despite political manouvering, measures continued in preparation for war. At first, the A.R.P. organisation was not taken very seriously by the general public. Some people even said that these precautions increased the likelihood of war! The Wandsworth Council however, forged ahead but made a scathing attack on the government about delays caused by 'red-tape' or, as Col. Dolland, in charge of Wandsworth's preparations, graphically put it, "wooden heads in brass hats".

Progress was being made on air-raid trenches and there were enough air-raid personnel for a 24 hour rota. Nine permanent shelters had been started in Wandsworth Park, with seven scheduled for Putney Lower Common and five for King George's Park. Not all went smoothly. The shelters on the north side of Clapham Common had been started in September 1938 and had still not been finished by November 1939. Two contractors had gone bankrupt but eventually a third finished the job. Later in the year it was decided to supplement these with 31 communal surface type, brick shelters, in areas where it was impossible to provide garden or basement shelters.

Over 5,000 basements had been surveyed and eventually 558 were selected as suitable. These were checked for electric lights, drinking water, gas and conduits. They had to be of adequate height and have reasonable access. They could accommodate 26,000 people, many who would come off the streets.

In Battersea, the Town Clerk, who was the controller of the local A.R.P., authorised the strengthening of the kitchen and chair-store in the Lower Town Hall, to be used as the reporting and communications centre.

Individual households also had to be catered for and this took the form of the Anderson shelter. It was estimated that Wandsworth needed 19,000, of which 3,000 had been delivered by May. The first shelters in Tooting arrived on the Totterdown Estate in March. Council workmen arrived early

CLAPHAM COMMON P
SHELTERS UNDER
CONSTRUCTION

PUBLIC SHELTER
CLAPHAM COMMON

one morning and the breakfast things were pushed to one side and the housework forgotten, as people went to watch the fun. The general opinion was that they were a 'necessary evil' and people were discussing what to do with them. Solutions were many and varied, ranging from garden sheds and chicken runs to tents and sun balconies. Some people did not want them at all.

The shelters came in a kit of 20 pieces, consisting of 14 steel plates and six girders, accompanied by a bag of nuts and bolts and a spanner. In some houses there was difficulty in reaching the back gardens and the workmen had to struggle to lift sections through windows. When constructed, the shelter measured $7\frac{1}{2}$ feet high, $6\frac{1}{2}$ feet long and $5\frac{1}{2}$ feet wide and was sunk about 4 feet into the ground with the remaining earth piled on top. As most gardens were quite small, the completed shelter took up a lot of space. When winter set in with the accompanying bad weather, some shelters had problems with flooding, especially in Southfields and Roehampton.

The A.R.P. organisation continued to train its personnel and then held joint exercises with neighbouring areas. On the night of Wednesday, 1st February, the most realistic and comprehensive air-raid practice so far held in South London, took place on Tooting Common. The scheme had been kept a strict secret and the public, until they heard the sirens, were unaware that anything unusual was to take place. The object of the exercise was to test the mobilisation and communications arrangements and to give members of the Auxiliary Fire Service and the A.R.P. some idea of their duties in time of war and to co-operate with the London Fire Brigade.

The exercise assumed that enemy planes had dropped bombs on and around the common. Warning of the "air-raid" was given by the police at 8.05pm, when they sounded the sirens. Ten minutes later, thirty-six fire calls were received and the firemen went into action. Other "fires" were left to be discovered by cycle patrols and air-raid wardens.

ANDERSON SHELTER

The area of the raid was bounded on the north by Battersea Rise, on the south by Tooting Junction, on the east by Tooting Bec Common and on the west be Earlsfield Station. Four roads were designated as being blocked by debris, these being Franciscan Road, Mellison Road, Chestnut Grove and Boundaries Road. The "fires" were graded to their seriousness, from those that could be dealt with by hand appliances, to those that required six appliances, up to the most serious needing forty-nine fire engines.

The final part of the exercise was a "serious fire" on Tooting Bec Common, where all fifty-two appliances were needed. Fire effects were simulated by searchlights covered with red cellophane and smoke bombs set off at the edge of the pond. Water was drawn from the pond and from two huge dams, which between them held 12,000 gallons of water. During the exercise, the water was pumped straight back into the source supply, so as not to flood the area.

Over 2,000 people took part, watched by thousands of spectators. Amongst them was the M.P., Herbert Morrison, who had closely followed the sequence of events, riding on one of the fire-engines up to the common. He arrived back at the Trinity Road headquarters with his coat liberally spattered with mud, but full of admiration for the efforts of the volunteers and the way the exercise was carried out.

As the year progressed more local exercises were carried out. One took place in Southfields on a Sunday morning in mid-May. A "bombing" car drove round the area, with a warden throwing out different coloured tennis balls. Each colour represented a different type of bomb, yellow and green denoting gas, red were high explosives and those with red stripes incendiary devices. The reporting centre in the basement of Putney Library, with its bank of 10 telephones, was soon a hive of activity. Plots were marked on a large-scale borough map and the required service given instructions.

In the Tooting Bec area, some wardens devised a board game. A counter was dropped on a map of their district, then a card was drawn from a special pack, which indicated the type of bomb and the damage caused. The warden 'on duty' then had to work out what to do. The idea proved popular and was taken up by other districts.

Another large exercise took place in June 1939, on Clapham Common, involving units of the different services from all over South London. It

AUXILIARY FIRE
TAXI PULLED TR
ELTRINGHAM S
WANDSWOR

was organised by the National Defence Public Interest Committee and started in the afternoon, continuing through to the evening.

Fighter planes of no. 601 County of London Squadron raided the common, diving low, pretending to drop bombs, disappearing and returning for a second time. The anti-aircraft units went into action, demonstrating their skills and a barrage balloon was launched, rising to a height of 1,000 feet. The A.F.S. dealt with incendiaries dropped by the aircraft, while the British Red Cross and the A.R.P. squads carried out various exercises. In the

evening the aircraft returned to allow the search-light and sound-locator crews to test their new equipment.

The thousands of spectators were entertained by the band of the Auxiliary Fire Service and there were static displays housed in a large marquee. The A.R.P. had an exhibition of "What to do and what not to do in an air-raid", models of gas-proof rooms and pictures of the bombing in Spain. There were also information and recruiting desks for all the voluntary services. Over 9,000 volunteers enrolled for the A.R.P., enough to cover the whole of the Borough of Wandsworth.

The same month, the results of Hitler's ruth-less policy against the Jews was brought to the notice of local residents. The Home for Aged Jews in Nightingale Lane had received many applications for places from German Jewish refugees, who had fled the persecutions, unable to bring much money or possessions with them. The Home agreed to take as many people as possible without reducing the normal numbers of beds usually available. The refugees were maintained by the German Jewish Aid Committee and the cost of the additional equip-

ment was defrayed privately by members of the Home's committee, to avoid depleting their general funds.

However, the policy to these unfortunate people was rather ambiguous, as shown by a case reported in the local paper of the arrest of a German Jew in October 1939. He was Gerhard Miedzwriska, a civil engineer, who had left his native Breslau and obtained an entry visa for Britain. This was on condition that he did not obtain work but it was found that he had been employed as an engineer and so it was recommended that he be deported. It is hard to understand today, why the authorities would want someone to live on charity when they were quite capable of supporting themselves, as well as helping in the war effort.

On the 1st August, Tooting received its first barrage balloon. It took to the air from the grounds of St. Benedict's Hospital but was hauled down in the afternoon as the cable was believed to be interfering with a nearby church tower.

COLIN CROCKER WITH HIS SISTER WITH 'PIRATE SHIP' SAIL MADE OF BLACKOUT MATERIAL, 1944

THE ANDERSON SHELTER
OFTEN SAVED LIVES

Also that month, a national blackout test took place. The Councils requested all wardens to volunteer to take part in the exercise. The men were to operate in pairs and after 12.30am, to knock at the door of any private house where unscreened lights were noticed. They were also to report lights showing in factories or illuminated advertising signs and finally to familiarise themselves with the topographical features of their sector under blackout conditions.

On the whole, the experiment was a success, where large buildings, such as Battersea Power Station, were able to keep in full production, without any light being visible outside. From the air it was noticed that buses were too brilliantly lit and that vehicles, even with only side-lights, indicated where the main roads in and out of London were situated.

The event was not without its lighter moments as reported by wardens in the Earlsfield area. One resident was unconvinced that the light from his house was illuminating the neighbouring playing fields. He insisted on judging for himself and carefully closed his front door behind him. Unfortunately, he had forgotten he was alone in the house and was seen later, climbing through an upper window. At another house, a kitchen was brilliantly lit and despite repeated knocking, the family slumbered on.

There seemed to be an air of unreality as the political situation worsened. The Mayor of Battersea, Cllr McIvor, decided to postpone a holiday trip to the Isle of Wight for 70 local girls, as the times were so uncertain. He hoped that in a week or two, they would be able to go but that was not to be. Very few children were playing on the commons, which normally would have been a hive of activity. Prisoners were transferred from Wormwood Scrubbs to Wandsworth Prison. The kerb-stones at street corners were painted white, traffic lights dimmed and council vehicles had their headlamps shrouded. Various main roads were designated as one-way in case of mass-evacuation. Evening newspaper sellers did a roaring trade as people were eager for the latest news.

On the 1st September, 1939, it was confirmed that Poland had been invaded and that an ultimatum had been given to the German government. On Sunday, 3rd September, everybody waited for the Prime Minister's broadcast. Just after he announced that war with Germany had been declared, the first air-raid warning sounded at 11.33am. People had been warned to expect the worst so they went to their nearest shelter. Those out in the street were invited into houses and Anderson shelters. At the Clapham Congregational Church, Grafton Square, the minister, the Rev. A. Halfpenny was so engrossed in his sermon that he did not hear the siren.

His congregation did but although some shifted uneasily in their seats, they remained where they were. It was a false alarm and the 'all-clear' sounded half-an-hour later.

The first test of 'nerves' came early on Monday morning, when another alert was sounded. Again nothing happened but it provided the local wardens with the opportunity of taking note as to how people reacted. Some went to their shelters, some remained in bed, while others made cups of tea and listened to the radio, as it was too early for the newspapers to have been delivered. One enterprising Tooting resident took the time to mow the lawn in his front garden.

Many changes occurred in those first few weeks. Shops were closing at dusk because of the black-out and one or two closed completely as the staff had joined the Armed Services. People were filling sandbags and digging trenches. Cinemas and theatres were closed until further notice and some libraries were closed as they were being used for war work. The evacuation of children had also been put into motion on that first Monday.

The Registrar's office at Wandsworth Town Hall had been inundated by couples wanting to get married. Long queues for application forms grew amongst the sand-bags forming a splinter proof corridor. The Marriage Room, beautifully decorated with summer flowers, worked overtime, conducting 20 to 30 marriages a day, although all were given the same individual, unhurried treatment. Many of the bridegrooms were due to be called up and many of the brides carried a gas-mask instead of a bouquet.

At first everyone took their gas-mask everywhere they went, as the fear of a gas attack had been ingrained on their minds for months. However, by the end of September people began to get careless. The London Transport lost property office had acquired nearly 2,000 gas-masks by this time and the pile was added to at a rate of 100 per day. Many were just labelled "Mum", "Dad" or "Jim".

Trains and buses were kept running normally, except for some cuts at off-peak periods. The windows on public transport were blacked-out, except for a small diamond shape in the centre of the glass. This and the dim, blue lighting at night, created great difficulty of seeing where you were. Many a time passengers went past their usual stop, unless a friendly conductor or guard sang out the name of the stop.

There was also a rise in street accidents at night due to the strict black-out conditions. Vehicles were only allowed to run on side-lights and these were usually shrouded in some sort of hood. Side roads were unlit and even hand torches could only be used if the glass was covered with two layers of tissue paper and held so as to point at the ground. Even then they were not supposed to be lit

continuously, only switched on at particularly difficult places. No wonder people tripped over the kerb-stones or banged into objects.

Magistrates took a dim view of drivers hitting other vehicles or injuring pedestrians and would not take the black-out as an excuse. The police and air-raid wardens strictly controlled the black-out from day one. Some people were obstinate and often obstructive when told about a light showing, leading to arguments and fights. An inspection from the top of Queenstown Road gasometer, showed that rear-windows, facing the railway tracks were lighting up the lines. Residents thinking that the wardens could not see the rear of their houses had been lax in fixing the black-out materials. The offenders were fined quite heavily but there were still many people being prosecuted in the following months.

After the declaration of war, both councils brought their A.R.P. plans into full operation, the Town Clerks heading the administration of the individual organisations. London was divided into nine groups and the local area consisted of Wandsworth, Battersea, Camberwell, Lambeth and Southwark. Wandsworth was divided into 6 divisions, each being sub-divided into groups and sectors. The Putney division, with a population of 72,000, was divided into 19 groups and 151 sectors. The 32 warden's reporting posts were situated about $\frac{1}{4}$ mile apart. Of these, 11 were situated in existing buildings, while 21 had to be specially built.

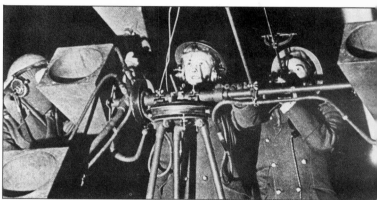

ANTI-AIRCRAFT SOUND LOCATORS

Each sector had six wardens, giving an establishment for the Borough of Wandsworth of 4,218 of whom 843 were paid personnel. Later in the war this number was giving cause for concern, as the cost was way over budget and the paid staff was reduced to 702.

The wardens, after inspecting any bomb damage, would fill out a report form, which would indicate the various follow-up services that were required. The units of the casualty services consisted of Light Rescue, Light and Heavy Mobile Units and First Aid Posts. The Light Rescue Parties were always early on the scene of an incident and as their name implies, performed rescue work of an easily accessible nature. In the early years of the war, they were known as the "Stretcher Party Service" and many casualties received first aid treatment from this unit. They also helped in loading and unloading casualty trains, clearance of incendiaries, furniture salvage and even assisted in the emergency distribution of coal.

Germans, Austrians and later Italians were interred for security reasons. The Royal Victoria Patriotic Asylum on Wandsworth Common was used for this purpose, the girl pupils having been evacuated to Hertfordshire. A Clapham barrister, Captain F.E. Sugden, was appointed to examine the position of refugees whose cases had been submitted by the police. He had to decide those who should be interned and those that could be exempt. Some had been settled in England many years but were still imprisoned, while others newly arrived were released. One wonders what happened to the former S.S. Trooper, Edward Ries, who lived on the Shaftesbury Park Estate in Battersea. Two weeks after the outbreak of war he married another refugee, Else Donneweg, at the Battersea Registry Office. In Germany, where his father owned a bakelite factory, he had been refused permission to marry because Else's mother was Jewish. He resigned from the S.S. and they both managed to reach Belgium, where they obtained a temporary visa to enter Britain.

The night of Friday, 29th September was fixed for the taking of the National Register census. Everyone who was in the house or normally lived there, was to be listed. The following day the forms were collected and shortly after the issuing of Identity Cards took place. The census was also used as a basis for a food rationing scheme. Along with rationing, prices were strictly controlled and severe penalties were to be imposed on profiteers. Price increases were allowed only if these could be shown to be due to a rise in the cost of raw materials, manufacture, transport, wages, insurance premiums and other causes sanctioned by the Board of Trade. There were many complaints in the two boroughs about price increases. A few of the new prices were found to be justified but most were ruled 'illegal'. The majority were mistakes occurring through bad management but some were shown to be where shop keepers were trying to make an extra profit.

Towards the end of September, it was realised that there was not going to be continued, devastating bombing, so the cinemas and theatres began to re-open. The staff at the Granada, Clapham Junction, had taken a course on A.R.P. precautions, so that they could cope during emergencies. The doorman reminded patrons without gas-masks, that they should carry them at all times, although none were refused entry. The Wandsworth and Wimbledon Stadiums started to hold greyhound race-meetings in the afternoons because of the blackout.

Except for the black-out, life continued nearly as normal throughout the winter of 1939-40. The Wimbledon Theatre had the usual Christmas pantomime, which that year was Cinderella. The libraries re-opened at the end of October and there was gread demand for Hitler's "Mein Kampf" and other books on Germany. One piece of bad news was that income tax was being raised to 7s. 6d. ($37\frac{1}{2}$p) in the £1, the highest level in the history of the tax.

INTERNEES IN THE GRO[...] OF THE ROYAL VICTORIA[...] PATRIOTIC ASYLUM, WANDSWORTH COMM[...] 1939

THE PHONEY WAR

At the outbreak of the war, the public were keen to fight against Hitler. They had seen the flood of Jewish and political refugees from Germany, Austria and Czechoslovakia. They studied maps of Poland but after a while began to wonder why the Government were not doing anything. By the beginning of 1940, there was a rising level of public dissatisfaction and apathy that began to cause concern.

High morale was important and the Government formed the Home Intelligence Unit. Officials on public transport, managers of large stores and cinemas, council officials, trade unionists and social workers, all reported regularly on Londoners' attitudes to the war. There were also secret sources from police duty room reports, as well as postal censorship. About two hundred thousand letters a month were checked to see if any unintentional leaking of military information was occurring as well as getting an insight about general attitudes to the war.

From the start there was a huge difference between people's real reactions and what was officially released in the newspapers or broadcast on the radio. Nobody foresaw the tidal wave of refugees invading places like Oxford; nobody foresaw that the rest centres would be overflowing, that people would stay there for weeks instead of hours, that people would not be billeted in their own area, that transport would not turn up, that people would flock to the Tube, in fact, there were rather too many things that nobody foresaw.

On land, the war had come to a virtual standstill, with Somerset Maugham providing an article to the local newspapers about a trip to the Maginot Line. At sea the U-boats and surface raiders had taken their toll but one morale booster was the rescue of British sailors from the "Altmark", a German ship sheltering in a Norwegian fjord. One of the seamen rescued was from Tooting, whose ship had been sunk by the "Graf Spee". Other sailors made a personal appearance on the stage of the Putney Palace cinema and later were entertained by the local residents.

On the home front, food rationing had started but only on bacon, butter and sugar. Coal was in short supply, especially in Balham and Tooting but the local M.P. was able to arrange a train load,

emergency supply. The local authorities were concerned about the number of black-out infringements, most caused by carelessness, although some offenders were clearly negligent. A survey also showed that only 1 person in 3 was carrying their gas-mask.

Another concern was the escalating cost of the A.R.P. services, estimated at £100,000 a year for Wandsworth alone. Under pressure from higher authority, Wandsworth Council reviewed the paid personnel and reluctantly reduced the numbers. The local residents were grumbling that the air-raid wardens were being paid £3 a week for doing nothing. However, the continual practices paid off when the 'Blitz' started, as everyone knew exactly what to do.

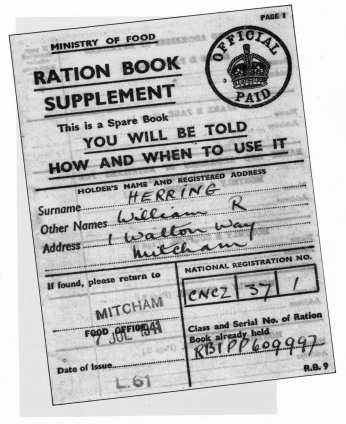

One such exercise was a mock air-raid on Clapham, with bombs plotted as having fallen in the Larkhall Lane-Union Grove area. Some derelict houses were used, with one 'casualty' being lowered in a bosun's chair from a first floor window. In Battersea, three houses in Sheepcote Lane were set on fire, with one made to collapse. The 'casualties' were dealt with at a disused warehouse in Lombard Road. Most of the Battersea A.R.P. men were involved, coming under the close scrutiny of the Mayor and Town Clerk.

In Wandsworth, the men were able to wash away the dust with a nice cup of tea dispensed from a new mobile canteen, which had been formally received by the Mayor, Cllr Bonney, in June. It had been specially designed and built for emergency work and paid for by local subscriptions. The canteen was built on a Ford V-Eight chassis and was equipped with a Calor gas supply able to supply hot drinks and snacks.

A further outcry over money was raised, when the Wandsworth Council announced it was to build a bomb-proof centre under the carpark at the rear of the Municipal Buildings at a cost of £15,000. The domestic rates had just been raised by 6d (2½p)

MOBILE CANTEEN PRESENTED BY THE PEOPLE OF ONTARIO. INSPECTED BY ADMIRAL SIR EDWARD EVANS

in the £1 and this additional cost angered many ratepayers. Larger companies had their own facilities, such as those at the Wandsworth Gas Works. They had reinforced the railway arches and erected tunnel and concrete shelters. The H.E. Jones Memorial Institute was turned into an A.R.P. headquarters, which included a first-aid post and a decontamination room. The works firestation had two fire tenders and 4,000 feet of hose, with a 'Foamit' plant for dealing with oil blazes. The station was manned by a crew of twelve, working in shifts with other helpers on call. Stockpiles of materials for repairing the mains were kept ready for any emergency.

Everybody became involved in the war and one of the tasks was the collection of salvagable materials, much of which had originally been imported. Woodpulp was a major item, so there was a massive drive to recycle waste paper. Paper and paperboard was being used by the armed forces for artillery shell cartons, packing of many items from rifles to food and the building of huts.

Two local firms on the Wandle, Stevenson and Son of the Corruganza Works, Summerstown and the New Merton Board Mills, were desperate for paper. Between them, they employed over 1,000 local people and required 400 tons of pulp per week. On one day the Corruganza Works were down to 4 hours supply. Waste paper had declined, as many firms had moved from London, newspapers had reduced in size and much of the packaging and cardboard boxes were being saved and reused. Even so, it was estimated that at the beginning of 1940 only a third of waste paper was being saved.

At first, collection was a very hit and miss affair, with boy scouts and other organisations doing the collection. By May, the Councils had been persuaded to undertake the collection but only after much argument and pressure from local businesses. Every household was asked to save scrap iron, steel, bones, glass, books and paper. Within a three week period the Women's Voluntary Service had collected 100 tons of scrap metal, 25 tons of paper and over 90,000 bottles. The dust carts had no special compartments for salvage, so everything had to be sorted at the Feather's Wharf depot. Iron railings started to disappear, those from Battersea Park being some of the first to go. It was estimated that some London streets had enough metal to make a dozen tanks.

The residents of Clapham started "comfort" parcels to send to local men serving in the armed services. The idea spread to other areas and the W.V.S. were soon busy putting together these packages. The contents included razor blades, toilet soap, shaving soap, toothpaste, chocolate, handkerchieves, balaclavas, scarves, socks, gloves, playing cards, writing paper with envelopes, games and reading matter. In five months, the clearing centre on East Hill dealt with nearly 13,000 items.

One import from America that took up no shipping space was the "Jitterbug" dance. By April, this new craze was sweeping the country and contests were held at the Locarno, Streatham and the Grand, Clapham Junction to find the best couples. No doubt the older generation shook their heads at this decadent exhibition.

On the military front, things were relatively quiet. The 1st Battalion 23rd London Regiment (T.A.), whose H.Q. was at St. John's Hill, Battersea, joined the British Expeditionary Force in France. Fighting broke out on the 9th April with the

German invasion of Denmark and Norway. This was followed by the attack on neutral Holland and Belgium. The Dutch army surrendered on the 15th May and Belgium only lasted a little longer.

The Battersea and Wandsworth Councils quickly made an appeal for people to register any spare accommodation for refugees, while they themselves rapidly renovated vacant council premises. The canvass drew a response of 5,000 promises of help.

The refugees soon began to arrive, being cleared through the Magdalen Hospital, Streatham, the Wimbledon Stadium and the Southlands Health Centre, Battersea. They came from towns and villages and all walks of life. Most had few belongings, some with bicycles, while others had only the clothes they were wearing. All had stories of being machine-gunned and bombed by the Luftwaffe, of families being split up, some killed, some just lost in the confusion. A Balham woman working as a dancer in Rotterdam, told of how she crawled through the streets with bombs falling everywhere. She boarded a ship, which was attacked several times but managed to reach England unscathed.

The first contact the local residents had with their new 'guests' was a knock at the door. Someone from the W.V.S. or a similar organisation then introduced the tired-faced, apprehensive people, clutching their few possessions and then returned for another group. The refugees were soon made at home but it must have been months before they recovered from their traumatic experiences.

As the war situation deteriorated, public attitudes changed from discontent to one of fighting and beating the Germans at all costs. However, a phobia developed against all foreigners and even some recently arrived refugees were badly treated. At the outbreak of war all known Nazi supporters and sympathisers had been interned. In May, 1940, all grade B suspects were rounded up, which included second-generation Italians or those who had arrived in Britain as young children.

After the retreat from Dunkirk, panic set in and all enemy aliens were interned, including many German and Austrian Jews, most of whom were eager to fight against Hitler. On the Henry Prince Estate, Garratt Lane, a near riot occurred when a middle-aged couple tried to distribute anti-government leaflets. It appears they were supporters of the Communist Party and the police had to escort them to safety, so angry had the tenants become at their anti-war sentiments.

The danger of invasion grew and the Government worried about German parachutists and airborne troops, hurriedly formed a new, voluntary, semi-military force, called the Local Defence Volunteers. Anthony Eden made a radio appeal for recruits and within hours there were long queues at police stations. The official age limits were 17 to 65, but there were recruits in their 80s, as well as 15 year olds. The original aim was for the L.D.V. to combat any small groups of parachutists, observe the movements of larger formations, block roads and to make sure any motor transport was immobilised. Instruction films were shown to recruits at local cinemas.

Companies were formed all over the two Boroughs, one of the first being at Balham. Four hundred men paraded at Fusilier House, Balham High Road and were formed into 5 companies and they included many who had served in the First World War. Their clothing varied from sports coats to business suits, the only 'uniform' issued being the L.D.V. armband. Very few fire-arms were available at first, being mainly shot-guns or antique rifles, with many of the men armed with a broom-handle with a kitchen knife bound to the end, forming a primitive bayonet.

Since the fall of France, the Luftwaffe had been attacking shipping in the Channel and the radar stations along the south coast. The R.A.F. had lost quite a number of aircraft over Europe and production was barely keeping up with losses. An appeal was made for aluminium utensils that could be used in the manufacture of aircraft. Local shops had special displays using parts of enemy aircraft or other objects such as German helmets.

All sorts of items were handed over, including aluminium saucepans, coffee percolators, colanders, coat hangers and even door knockers.

EVACUEES

The Government had decided that there was not to be any mass evacuation from London but it would help the 1,300,000 children and accompanying adults to leave the capital. It was a task of great magnitude and complexity, which had no precedent. The largest group would be school parties, who accounted for nearly half of the total, while nearly as numerous were the under fives. The latter presented the biggest problem as they each needed to be accompanied by the mother or another suitable adult.

The authorities had no idea of how many parents wanted their children evacuated, so they were asked to register at their local schools on May 19th and 20th, 1939. Expectant mothers were to receive priority, the children and then the blind. Most would be billeted in private houses but those with special needs were to be kept together.

At the end of August, the children went back to school one day early, to rehearse the evacuation procedure. On this particular morning the children did not "creep unwillingly to school" with their satchels but hurried along laden with their gas-mask, a change of underclothes, night-wear, toilet things, plimsoles, spare socks and sandwiches for the day, packed in suitcases, haversacks and parcels. The children were also supposed to wear a warm coat and, on inspection, most children seemed well equipped. However, one small boy arrived at school without a jacket and his only luggage was a gas-mask.

The scene at Lavender Hill School, Battersea, was typical of many others The children began to arrive at 8.30am, with all their paraphernalia. By 10.15am, three hundred pupils were lined up ready for departure, surrounded by many of the mothers, the teachers and other helpers. Problems were raised, discussed and disposed of, while the children passed the time by playing games. At 4.30pm, the children were sent home, leaving their bundles at the school.

After the declaration of war, the evacuation for real was started. At Tooting, the procedure seemed to go without a hitch. The children had reported at their schools very early, the first being Tooting Graveney School which opened by 6.20am. Two hours later they set off for Tooting Junction,

while shortly after the column from Broadwater School started for Haydon's Road Station accompanied by the headmaster and headmistress.

Tooting Junction was the old station for the village and for years had seen the start of Sunday school trips and seaside outings. The children were laughing and singing as they carried their belongings in all sorts of bags, attache-cases and brown paper parcels. Two small children were struggling along with a bag made from a mattress cover.

Outside the station, the ice-cream sellers were doing a roaring trade and many of the children had been given fruit and sweets by local well-wishers.

At last, with the children waving and last-minute instructions being shouted by anxious parents, the train set off for its various destinations amongst the South Downs and along the coast. At this time an invasion by the Germans seemed totally impossible.

Portrayed as a happy adventure by the authorities, there were often tearful partings with worried mothers not knowing when they would see their off-spring again or where they were going. For the children, after the first excitement of the 'holiday' had worn off, there was the anxiety of leaving home, which grew the longer the journey lasted. Then there was the trauma of being selected for a new home. It was often like a slave-market, where the able-bodied older boys were snapped up, especially in farming areas, as they provided un-

CHILDREN AWAIT EVACUATION IN SCH PLAYGROUND

20

paid labour. Neatly dressed children also did not have to wait long. There were complaints about the bad health of the children, about the vermin, dirt, bad language and behaviour and lack of clothing and money.

Doreen Holloway of Battersea remembers after arriving at Binfield in Berkshire, how it seemed that she and her brother William were rejects. Nobody wanted a couple but they refused to be separated. Eventually they were taken to a large house in the village. They were put in the care of two servants, who resented the intrusion, and had to sleep on straw-filled sacks although there were spare beds available. There were many petty restrictions and they were begrudged the food they were given. On visits, their parents were never allowed into the house, so no wonder they longed to go back to London with their Mum and Dad.

Not all children had such a bad experience and many, especially those on the coast, thought of it as an extended summer holiday. Postcards had been given to the children to post on arrival, to set their mothers' minds at rest. Three children from Wickersley Road, Battersea, ended up in Hove. The two sisters and the brother soon settled in, the latter helping his new 'Uncle' install his Anderson shelter.

Tom Smith of St. Josephs R.C. School, Battersea, wrote on his postcard:- "I am having a good time by the sea. The lady is kind to us and nice. There are four of us in the house. Bed at seven. I can't write anything more. Your loving son, Tommie." Other children from St. Mary's and Plough Road Schools, Battersea, seemed to be having a lively time, as they were wearing out plimsolls and socks at a great rate. An appeal had to be made to parents for additional shoes and clothes.

Parents tried to keep regular contact with their children and the Sunday morning excursion trains to the South Coast were always packed. However, some Tooting mothers were not so lucky as their off-spring had been sent 170 miles away, to the villages of Winsford and Dulverton in Somerset. There were cheap train fares of 12s 6d to Taunton, but the additional 30 mile taxi ride to the villages added another 30 shillings, which few could afford. One couple spent a total travelling time of seven hours to have sixty minutes with their children, before starting the return journey.

The Mayor of Battersea, Cllr McIver, visited the children of Mantua Street School, who had gone to the Reading area in Berkshire. One stop was at the estate of Sir George and Lady Leon, where an old cottage had been converted into an eight-bed hospital for the evacuees. A large barn had been equipped as a play centre-handicraft room and $1\frac{1}{2}$ acres of land had been handed over to the boys, who had planted 200 cabbages. Although well cared for, the Mayor was concerned that a few

children were sleeping on strawfilled mattresses on the floor.

Earlsfield Senior School had been evacuated to "somewhere in Surrey" and their experiences of settling in were typical of many schools. The first two weeks were spent mainly out of doors, the boys starting each day with a session of physical exercises. They then explored the surrounding countryside and during the ramble, nature-study, biology, geology, geographic features and other subjects were informally discussed. The continuing good weather, the fresh air and regular meals had a beneficial effect on most of the children, who seemed to expand both physically and mentally.

THE FIRST "WAVE" OF CHILDREN TO EVACUATE 1st SEPTEMBER 1939
Illustrated London News

Real schooling started on September 18th when they were allocated classrooms in the local, central school, for the afternoon sessions. The mornings were devoted to assembly, drill and briefings on that day's walk, followed in the afternoons by lessons in the "three Rs". When the weather was too bad for outdoor activities, two halls were used for recreational activities, such as singing, dancing, drama, needlework and handicrafts.

Some smaller or private schools had problems with a falling number of pupils. Putney High School had been evacuated to Reading. Many of its pupils came from the outer 'neutral' areas of London, such as Kingston and Richmond and as their local schools were re-opening, some parents were withdrawing their daughters. Eventually permission was given for the school to return to Putney but had to use temporary premises in the Upper Richmond Road, as their school buildings had been taken over by the Metropolitan Police. The younger girls stayed at Caversham in case evacuation again became necessary.

As Christmas drew near, it was proposed that the Borough Council should contribute to a special fund to ensure that all the children away from home had as happy an occasion as possible. The pupils from Sellincourt Road School, Tooting, who had been evacuated to the Chichester area, were taken to a party at a local school. The tea consisted of sandwiches, a sausage roll, a mince pie, a bag of crisps and a bottle of milk, followed by the usual party games.

One group of children at Selsey, were delighted by a surprise visit from the Queen. A Tooting girl, Jean Boniface, was chosen to present the Royal bouquet and immediately afterwards wrote a letter home with the exciting news.

Another Royal visit had taken place the previous month, when the Queen made an unscheduled visit to the Balham Nursery School, which had been housed at Chelwood Gate, Sussex, the home of the M.P. Harold MacMillan. The bouquet on this occasion was presented by four-year old Tony Nolan.

Despite the many reunions planned for Christmas and the warnings that just because the bombs had not 'rained down' so far, it was still not safe to return, many mothers were unhappy about the length of time that their children were likely to be away. There began a drift back to the capital and by Christmas 1939, over half the evacuees had returned to London.

Some children became 'homesick', especially as some parents could not afford the cost of the fares and the heeding that war-time slogan, "Is your journey really necessary?". One 12 year old in Wolverton, Buckinghamshire, decided to visit his home in Tooting, 58 miles away. Early one morning he started his walk home. Fortunately, after about 5 miles, he was picked up by a friendly lorry driver, who on arrival in London treated the lad to breakfast and the fare to Tooting. On arrival at home, the boy explained to his startled mother: "As you have not been to see me, I've come to see you."

By February 1940, a large number of children had returned home and as there were no schools open, they were roaming the streets and not receiving any education. 'Gangs' were fighting each other and there were many acts of burglary and theft. Voluntary youth centres were opened in church halls and there was a good response from the children. Eventually, the London County Council decided to open some buildings as emergency schools. Admission, at first, was restricted to those between the ages of 11 and 16 years, but younger children were admitted when places could be found. Each child was restricted to lessons either in the morning or afternoon on alternate weeks.

In the event of an air-raid, the children would be taken to the safest place in the building and the outer gate would be shut. If the raids became serious or frequent, the schools would again be closed. Parents were repeatedly urged not to bring children back to London, as the full curriculum could not be provided.

There was a new appeal in March, for children under 5 to be registered for evacuation. This would only take place if air-raids made it necessary. The parents had to sign an undertaking that when the children left with a school party, they would stay away until officially allowed to return. By June, the scheme had to be put into action as the war situation worsened and over 4,000 children from Battersea and Clapham were sent to South Wales and the West Country.

Most children were well looked after and settled down with their "foster parents". Three Wandsworth girls at Werlham in Somerset were induced to put 6d a week away for savings certificates. Those much farther away from home had little choice but had to be content to stay where they were. It was not until 1945 that they returned to London, no doubt confused for a time by the strangeness and the changes caused by the bombing. Street victory parties helped them to settle back home.

THE GREAT "TREK" TO THE COUNTRY 9th SEPTEMBER 1939
Illustrated London News

THE BLITZ
AUGUST 1940–MAY 1941

In August, the Mayor of Wandsworth announced the opening of a Spitfire fund. Each fighter was nominally priced at £5,000 and a bomber £20,000. Battersea's mayor hoped to pay for a bomber but a Spitfire would do. In Wandsworth, the aim was one Spitfire from each of the political divisions. The first subscriber in Balham and Tooting was the local M.P., Sir Alfred Butt, who gave 100 guineas (£105) and over £400 was raised in one week.

All sorts of ways were thought up for raising money. There were collections door-to-door, in cinemas and private donations - a war widow gave £2 made up in farthings. Captured, barely damaged, enemy aircraft were put on show and an entrance fee charged for a close look, usually 6d for adults and 3d for children. A Heinkel bomber was put on show in the car park of the Granada Cinema,

Tooting and a Messerschmitt Me 109 fighter did a tour of the Wandsworth Greyhound Stadium, the southside of Clapham Common and the car park of the Golden Domes, Streatham, at the rear of the Post Office. These aircraft aroused a great interest and quite a sum was raised in this manner for the Spitfire fund.

When the appeal was closed in November, 1940, sufficient money was raised for three aircraft. The actual machines and the names they bore were as follows: Spitfire Vc, MA 281, Wandsworth (Clapham, Balham & Tooting Divisions). This was allocated to 33 Maintenance Unit on 18th May 1943 and to 82 MU at Casablanca on the 1st June that year. It was struck off the serviceability

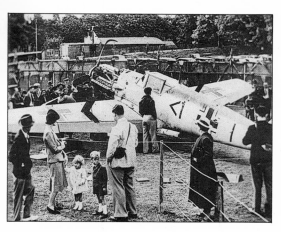

INSPECTING A MESSERSCHMIDT 109E
Illustrated London News

A WANDSWORTH SPITFIRE VC

list on 16th September 1944. Spitfire Va/Vb, W 3766, Wandsworth (Putney, Roehampton & South-fields). Allocated to 222 Squadron (code ZD) on 21st January 1943 and based at Ayr, flying convoy patrols. It was transferred to 64 Squadron on 31st March 1943, also based at Ayr, (code SH), on convoy patrol and practising carrier landings on H.M.S. Argus. In August 1943 64 Squadron moved south to Friston and thence to Gravesend in September that year. W 3766 passed to 118 Squadron (NK) on 25th September 1943, soon travelling north again to Peterhead and Castletown in October 1943. In January 1944 they moved on to Detling in Kent to be converted to Spitfire IX. W 3766 was then handed over to 6 Maintenance Unit in the north and passed on to 61 OTU on 2nd August 1944, being written off as unserviceable on 10th May 1945. Spitfire Va/Vb, W3767, Wandsworth (Streatham & Central Divisions). This aircraft was allocated to 8 MU on 19th August 1941, passing on to 609 Squadron (code PR) on 22nd August that year. The latter was the "West Riding Auxiliary Squadron", stationed at Gravesend from July to September 1941, moving to Biggin Hill some time in September. W 3767 went missing on 17th September 1941 after just four weeks in service during the aerial battle for Britain.

As the summer progressed, the battle in the skies gradually drew nearer to London. On the 15th August, Croydon Airport was attacked and the noise of the bombing could be heard from South West London. Colin Perry, in his book "Boy in the Blitz", describes what he could see and hear from the top of the flats, Holmbury Court, Tooting, where he lived:

"Standing on the window-sill of the top floor landing, I looked out over Surrey. There over Croydon were a pack of planes, so tiny and practically invisible in the haze, and by God!, the Hun was bombing Croydon Airport. Machine-guns rattled over the still air and there, only a few miles away, bombs commenced to drop. Anti-aircraft guns threw a dark ring around the darting planes, Spitfires and Hurricanes roared to battle. A terrific cloud of smoke ascended from the town, two more fires, obviously slight, rose on the wind. Boy this was IT!"

Although London was not an official target, a number of bombs were dropped on the Metropolitan area. This meant that the air-raid sirens were being sounded, although no bombs fell. At the Granada, Clapham Junction, with an audience of 700, they continued to show films during the alert, plus the feature films from the previous week, several shorts and organised an amateur concert until the all-clear sounded, all for the regular price of 6d ($2^1/_2$p).

Street shelters varied in comfort and Mrs Alexander of Bennerley Road, Battersea, recalls that the ones nearest her house were not very savoury. Toilet facilities consisted of a bucket in a corner, with a sacking screen for modesty. The smell of urine, beer and cigarette smoke was rather overpowering and the family decided to stay put in their house. Mr Alexander removed the coal from the small room under the stairs, often the safest place, and put it in the garden. He lined it with sacking, put in a mattress with an eiderdown quilt and two orange boxes sawn in half to make seats and a table.

THE DEFENCES: SEARCHLIGHTS AND BALLOON 1940

INCH ANTI-AIRCRAFT
IS, CLAPHAM COMMON
rial War Museum

Other shelters were better organised and more comfortable. One local resident would bring in a wind-up gramaphone, another records and others would provide a spirit-stove, saucepans and kettle to provide soup and tea. Mr Pluchino of West Side Wandsworth Common, remembers how his father used to take his cine-projector to the shelter in Trefoil Road, showing Mickey Mouse cartoons to help keep everyones minds off the bombing. His father also explained to him about all the strange noises; about the aircraft, the bombs, the flack and the searchlights, which to a 3 year old seemed like a giant firework display.

After the bombing of London, the R.A.F. retaliated with an attack on Berlin. Hitler was outraged and ordered his bombers to concentrate on London. This took the pressure off the Fighter Command airfields and put the German escort fighters at a disadvantage. The pilots had to watch the fuel-gauges as they were operating at the extreme edge of their combat range.

The defences were waiting and consisted of barrage balloons and anti-aircraft batteries with their associated equipment. The balloons were to make aircraft fly at a higher level and so be less accurate in their bombing. The gas bags were attached to a winch by a long metal cable, which in turn was usually mounted on a lorry. Manned by R.A.F. personnel, they were dotted about in open spaces, such as the commons, parks, sports fields and later even bomb sites. The balloons had to be brought down in high winds as they tended to break loose and the trailing wire damaged many rooftops.

The anti-aircraft sites consisted of a battery of three or four guns partly sunk into protective emplacements. Those on Clapham Common and in Richmond Park were of 3.7 inch calibre and those near the windmill on Wimbledon Common were reused 5.25 inch twin-turrets from a 'Dido' class cruiser. In Battersea Park and on Tooting Bec Common were batteries of sixtyfour, twin 5 inch rockets, mounted on projectile launchers. The rockets exploded in a pattern like a more lethal version of a pellet-spray from a shotgun.

Before the heavy guns were fired, the position, range and height of the raider had to be calculated. Data was fed into the 'Predictor', an early form of computer, which supplied a series of possible positions of the enemy aircraft. The guns were then fired in a pattern as laid down by the predictor. The lighter support guns, the two-pounders and Lewis guns were used against low flying planes and were aimed by the gunners. At night, things were more difficult and searchlights criss-crossed the sky trying to pin-point the bomber. The work was aided by sound-locators which were not very accurate and depended much on the skill of the operator.

The first bomb on our area fell on the 2nd September, 1940, making a new bunker on the 16th fairway of the Roehampton Club golf course. The main attack came on the 7th September. It was a fine Saturday afternoon, when at 5pm, a wave of 300 bombers, escorted by 75 fighters, attacked, mainly over East London. This was followed two hours later by another wave of 250 bombers, guided by the fires started earlier. The palls of smoke also attracted numerous sight-seers. An appeal had to be made for these people to stay away as they were hindering the rescue services.

Battersea and Streatham bore the brunt of the local attacks on that day. Battersea was a prime target, with its great network of railway lines and goods-yards, two power stations, a gas works, factories, of which many were engaged in war-work, wharves and warehouses. The railway was attacked many times, as the line passing through the old village was one of the few direct links from the industrial North to the South coast and the Channel ports. Some lines were put out of action but never more than three days at one time. At Nine Elms, the roof of a signal-box controlling twelve tracks, was blown off by a blast but continued to operate.

One bomb fell on a street shelter in Rawson Street, near the junction with Battersea Park Road. Thirteen people were killed and four badly injured. The crater and rubble blocked both roads and many nearby shops were damaged.

It took all the next day to clear the main road and it was not until the 9th September, that the glass and debris were cleared from Rawson Street.

On the evening of Sunday, 8th September, the bombing continued for over nine hours, with Battersea suffering the heaviest blows. Putney received its first attacks, when bombs landed in the grounds of the Putney Lawn Tennis Club, on Puttocks Garage and the police station in Upper Richmond Road. Mr Geoffrey Haines, the Incident Officer for Putney, hurried to the police station ready to call out the rescue services but received a cool reception, being told they could look after themselves.

The following day, the police station was hit again. This time there were casualties and Mr Haines was received with open arms, the inspector being rather ashamed of the way he had been treated the day before. Opposite the police station was Mathias' drapery store, which had a reinforced basement shelter capable of holding nearly 200 people. The shop received a direct hit but the shelter was so effective that no one was injured. By March 1941, they were back in business.

The bombing continued night after night, reaching a peak in the middle of the month. On the three days, 14-16th September, Battersea had nearly 200 high-explosive bombs dropped, compared with 53 on the Borough of Wandsworth. The strong moonlight on Sunday 15th September made the night nearly as bright as day. Just before midnight, showers of incendiaries fell over Tooting. The roads were soon strewn with hoses as the Fire Service got to work. Motors whined, water jets

IRONIC FILM POSTER, BALHAM ODEON, OCTOBER 1940

swished, accompanied by the cracking of timbers and the crashing of walls. A.A. gunfire and distant explosions added to the din. By daylight the fires were out, leaving smoking ruins and rubble filled streets.

Over this period, there were many stories of tragedies, humorous events, miracles and calm amidst the chaos. One German bomber pilot bailed out and landed on a roof in the Clapham Park area. To the astonishment of the residents, who were sheltering in their cellar, he appeared at the top of the stairs repeating, "Police! Police" London!", the only English words he knew. At Balham, another airman was captured by the Home Guard. At Wandsworth County Court, Judge Haydon, K.C. refused to adjourn when the sirens sounded and by the time of the "All-clear", had satisfactorily concluded several cases. Johnny Peters, a well-known Battersea boxer, survived when his lorry carrying a road repair gang was thrown over a house by a bomb blast. It was 8 months before he was fit enough to return home. A 14 year old girl was rescued after her faint cries were heard coming from the rubble of her house, demolished four days previously.

At Tooting, one bomb buried itself deep in a back garden. Wardens rushed into the house and found a woman preparing Sunday lunch. In answer to their anxious questions, she replied that she was all right but something was wrong with the gas, as there was no pressure. In Wandsworth High Street, the "Old Bull" public house, next to the Wandle, was hit. "Pity it wasn't the old town hall", said one spectator with a dry sense-of-humour. "They want a new building and that bomb might have done a bit of good, but then, Jerry don't oblige like that!"

Another bomb landed in the cellar of a Balham club, smashing several hundred glasses and ten barrels of beer. The Battersea Town Hall had a near miss, when a bomb made a large crater in the road outside. Ornamental stone work and the balustrade over the entrance were brought down in the blast. The Mayor was visiting the Town Clerk at the time and both were shaken but unhurt. The official car, however, had been blown over onto the pavement and damaged beyond repair.

One night in October, a bomb exploded in Charlmont Road, Tooting, outside the premises of the Tooting and Balham Gazette, a local newspaper. The heavy front door was blown from its hinges and shrapnel sliced through a big safe, reducing the large ledgers inside to pulp. The works to the rear of the premises had the roof lights shattered, scattering splintered glass all over the printing machinery, to say nothing of the havoc created by the hundreds of scattered cases of loose type. After a considerable amount of labour in clearing glass and debris, there was time enough to print the next weekly issue as usual.

...M HILL, OCTOBER 1940

At about 8pm, a large, high explosive bomb penetrated the High Road, exploded beneath the surface, creating a high crater outside the United Dairies shop. Patrons at a nearby cinema were asked if they wanted to leave after the building had been rocked by the blast, causing plaster dust to shower down from the ceiling. Most stayed, so it was only later that they found out what had happened outside.

When it exploded, the bomb blew a hole through the roof of the north-bound platform, also severing the water and gas mains, as well as fracturing a sewer. Almost immediately, water began to trickle through the roof. Within minutes it was like a strong, flowing river, bringing tons of sand and rubble down on the 500 or so people sheltering in the station. The lights fused and the platforms plunged into darkness. A London Transport motorman, sheltering there with his family, fortunately knew the lay-out and with the aid of a torch, shepherded many people to safety.

At the height of the 'Blitz', the Government issued an appeal asking people to refrain from using the Underground stations as shelters, as it impeded the flow of passengers and disrupted the service. However, the public continued to use the deep lines and at nights every available space was used. This was to have a disasterous effect at Balham on the evening of the 14th October.

Above ground a number 88 bus was driving slowly along Balham High Road when the bomb exploded 25 yards ahead. Later the driver said, "the bus began prancing about like a horse and the next thing I knew was that I was lying in a shop doorway. After leaving a first aid post, I went back to my bus.

BALHAM TUBE 'INCIDENT'
14th OCTOBER 1940

"At first I thought somebody had moved it but when I got closer, I saw to my horror, that only the roof was protruding from the crater." Fortunately, the bus had only contained the crew, the conductor suffering mild concussion. Many of those below ground were not so lucky and 64 of the shelterers were killed.

It was not until Christmas that the last of the dead were removed and the rail line was out of action until January, 1941. The tramlines had also been destroyed and special cross-over points had to be installed at Ramsden Road and the Tooting side of the railway bridge. Once again the rescue services were soon on the scene and hard at work. All the training had paid off and people no longer grumbled about the waste of money.

THE BLOCKED TUNNEL,
BALHAM TUBE STATION.
16th OCTOBER 1940

Typical of what happened to many individual families is graphically described in the following account of Mrs Frost, at the time a teenager, at St Ann's Hill, Wandsworth.

"It became routine after our evening meal, to put on our night clothes and dressing-gowns, because once the warning siren went we never knew how long we would spend sheltering, check that we had torches, important papers and documents and something to keep us occupied, usually it was knitting.

This particular evening, Father was later home from work than usual and although the siren had sounded, Mother would not take cover until we were all together. After his arrival, when we were checking on all that was needed for that evening, we were having a discussion on whether one would hear the whistle of a bomb, should there be a direct hit on the house. A girl who was staying with us said she had been told that it wouldn't be heard and who were we to dispute it!

Father had just returned from outside, when we all felt an awful grinding or boring sensation, like a mammoth drill driving into the foundations of the house. The next thing was the lights going out. We were in the semi-basement of the house and I knew that in the room above was a three-piece suite, a dining table and a piano, all large enough to kill us if they dropped through the floor.

It seems hard to believe that there were no shouts or screams from anyone in the room. When it seemed there was nothing else coming down, the silence was broken by Mother's voice asking if anyone was hurt. When we convinced her we were all in one piece, she told us her leg was trapped.

The damage had been caused by an H.E. bomb that sliced a corner off the house and demolished some small houses opposite, with incendiaries setting fire to some timber stored in a yard. Apparently, after the primary blast, a suction action takes place. This had toppled a cupboard on top of which was my sister's piano-accordian and it was this that had landed on my Mother's leg, resulting in a fractured ankle. As a music lover, she took some ribbing over the incident as we all thought it was carrying things too far!

The first priority was to get out in case there was a fire. After fumbling in the dark, my Father found the door but it was jammed. However, the A.R.P. team were soon on the spot and ironically we were led up a mound of rubble and through a hole where once a wall had been – and we had been trying to find the door for an exit!

We were taken into a nearby public house and Mother went off to hospital. Some members of the local boys club suggested we go to their club room for the night. This we did but left again, when another bomb fell nearby. Then we returned to our Anderson shelter but found this was gradually filling up with water and there was escaping gas. So, still clad in nightwear, we tramped along to a friend's house for the night.

As we had helped ourselves, the local centre had no record of our whereabouts. An Aunt, who arrived the next day was very shocked when she saw the devastation. She had come to say that an Uncle and his family had been killed in the Balham Tube Station a few days before. After a short stay with my married brother at Wimbledon, we moved into a rented house in Cicada Road.

REPAIRING GAS MAIN
WEST HILL, WANDSW

DAMAGE TO TRAM LINE,
ST. JOHN'S HILL, BATTERSEA.
OCTOBER 1940. *L.T.E.*

Until we could salvage some of our furniture, we just had dresser drawers to sit on and until the council helped out with bare essentials, it was all quite primitive. Also, after a lot of persuasion, Father agreed to accept a bedroom suite that belonged to the relatives who had been killed. Weren't we thankful we all had a sense of humour and a sense of gratitude that we were still together."

Freaks caused by concussion and blast following bomb explosions were a common sight. A house which had been partly demolished, had pictures hanging on the wall, the glass still intact. A mirror and a number of ornaments, apart from

BOX OF THE LONDON
ENCE LINE, PUTNEY
WAY BRIDGE, 1940

being covered in dust, were unharmed. In another house, only the stairs remained; under the stairs was often a safe place to shelter. Cellars survived, holding back tons of rubble from those sheltering below.

One of the strangest things was the behaviour of windows. Some in the immediate vicinity of an explosion remained intact, yet others at a distance, caved in and shattered. In one road, a bomb blast had sliced off the gable ends of two houses. The bedrooms were quite unharmed, with beds, linen and furniture all neatly in place. A.R.P. workers too had lucky escapes. One Tooting group were bowled over by a blast and although covered in dust and debris, were unhurt.

After a raid, people tried to get back to normal as soon as possible. Odd pieces of lino, carpet, cardboard were used to cover gaps in window and shop fronts. The staff at Arding & Hobbs, Clapham Junction, cleared broken glass and debris caused by a near miss and it was business as usual, the store opening at the normal time. Family shops had numerous notices on their boarded-up fronts, saying that they were open.

The German raids continued through October and November, some areas only receiving the bomb load of a single plane, while Central Wandsworth and Battersea continued to receive more concentrated attention. The old 'Southlands' house at Battersea was completely destroyed and Queen Mary's Hospital at Roehampton had a near miss on the 29th October. A high explosive bomb landed near huts being used to manufacture artificial limbs for ex-servicemen. Since 1914, nearly 30,000 men had been helped, one famous patient being Douglas Bader. he lost both legs in a pre-war air crash but went on to fight as a pilot in the Battle of Britain.

In November, the bombers also turned their attention to cities in the rest of Britain. On the 14th, Coventry, a city of 250,000 population and many workshops was bombed for eleven hours. Over 600 tons of high explosives and thousands of incendiaries were dropped, simply blotting out the centre of the city, reducing the cathedral to ruins. Other cities and ports all around the country also suffered. Two nights later, on the 16th, during a heavy raid, the old Wandsworth Fire Station was hit by an 'oil-bomb', badly damaging the building and starting a fierce blaze.

On that night both the red appliances, the pump and the pump escape, were in the station and the crews resting, mainly in the basement of the building. Also in the basement was the control room, staffed largely by female personnel. On the ground floor was the watchroom with three officers and on the other side of the appliance room was the recreation room, where five firemen were resting.

When the bomb hit it killed the men in the watchroom, set fire to the fire engines and collapsed the recreation room side of the building, killing three of the firemen. The two others had a lucky escape, shielded from the debris by the strong legs and slate top of the billiard table, under which they had been sleeping. The staff in the basement were able to escape through an emergency hatchway into the station yard. Assistance was soon at hand, as the pumps from Battersea were already on their way to Wandsworth, when the incident took place. They got to work on the fire and rescue

operations commenced as soon as it was known that there were trapped survivors. Part of the building was temporarily reinstated in 1942, and lasted until 1955 when the new station was built.

Tooting Broadway was hit by several H.E. bombs, one landing in the middle of Mitcham Road, smashing the tram tracks like matchsticks. The walls of the Granada Cinema were pitted by bomb splinters but most of the light bulbs around the entrance were left intact. The library only had a single broken window but the memorial clock had one of its faces shattered, the hands stopped shortly before midnight. A nearby jewellery shop had its window display scattered into the road but on stocktaking afterwards, it was found that all the items had been collected by the staff or handed in by the public.

Sadly, this was not always the case and despite the wartime spirit of 'pulling together', there were many cases of looting and burglaries occurring while people were taking shelter. There were also a growing number of thefts of wholesale foods and goods, especially cigarettes, to service the 'black-market'. Bombed and damaged houses were looted and in some cases completely stripped of their contents.

THE PRE-WAR AND THE 'BLITZED' FIRE STATION, WEST HILL, WANDSWORTH. NOVEMBER 1940

'ON CHURCHILL VISITS
ELMS 1940

Mr Young of Summerley Street, Wandsworth, was granted 48 hours leave from the army to see to his bombed house. He found everything had gone, including his wife's and baby's clothes, who had been evacuated to the West Country. After a trip to the Town Hall, he was invited to a cup of tea by a local A.R.P. worker. To his astonishment and growing anger, he saw his own carpet in the hall, was served tea in his own cups and then spotted his canteen of cutlery on a sideboard. That was all he ever recovered of his property!

Many people were caught taking timber from demolished houses, which belonged to the local authority, to use in shoring up damaged buildings. Coal was another popular form of loot, although other things such as hats and door mats were taken as well. The courts were hard on offenders. In theory, people could be shot for looting but most were heavily fined, although one woman was sentenced to ten weeks hard labour. During December 1940, the German attacks grew less as the weather deteriorated and for two weeks over the Christmas period there was no bombing at all. This allowed some sort of festivities to take place but with rationing and shortages, most Christmas meals were rather basic. The Government had also laid on extra supplies of coal, topping up the local depots.

On the 29th December, the bombers returned with a vengeance, concentrating mainly on the City. St. Paul's Cathedral was clearly visible in a sea of flames and the Guildhall was severely dam-

aged. Another lull occurred over the New Year but people did not have much to celebrate. The sheer scale of the attack made people feel that London would soon be a heap of rubble. Several Underground stations had been hit, as well as a number of large shelters, causing many casualties.

The propaganda slogan "London can take it!" began to lose its impact and a top secret report recorded a lowering of morale. During daylight, the R.A.F had been able to intercept the enemy but at night it was a different matter. Night fighters, with a primitive, experimental radar, were few and made little impact. The anti-aircraft units had little chance of hitting the raiders but it did make them bomb from a greater height and the noise of the guns gave comfort to the sheltering Londoners. At least the threat of invasion had receded until the Spring.

One major concern was the hundreds of houses being destroyed or badly damaged. The local councils were responsible for those made homeless but as yet the system was inefficient. After a raid, the people were directed to collecting centres, where food and temporary shelter were available. Any who could not go to friends or relatives were then taken to rest centres, which were mainly at local schools and colleges. Camp beds were provided and washing and toilet facilities were on hand. People were encouraged to return home as soon as possible but if needed, they could be billeted with another local household.

Furniture salvaged from bombed premises was stored by the council until it could be transferred to the new home. They also helped wlth payments for those who needed to buy new furniture or clothes. Emergency repairs were made to houses but not to shops or commercial premises, unless they were essential to the welfare of the civilian population. The gas, electricity and water companies soon arrived after an incident, often working under dangerous and difficult conditions, restoring the services, mainly within twenty-four hours.

As in all bureaucratic societies, not all things went smoothly and sometimes there was a delay in the repair of homes. After much debate, the Wandsworth Council decided that the householder could get a builder to do basic repairs first and then submit the bill afterwards. A great debate was also going on, as to whether the council should modify some of the street lamps so that some of the side roads could be lit, or to continue to leave them switched off. Opponents to the scheme said that the money involved would pay for six Spitfires and others suggested that the unused lamp standards should be used for scrap metal. However, the proposal was carried by two votes and the lights were modified so as not to be visible from the air, making life a little more bearable during the winter months.

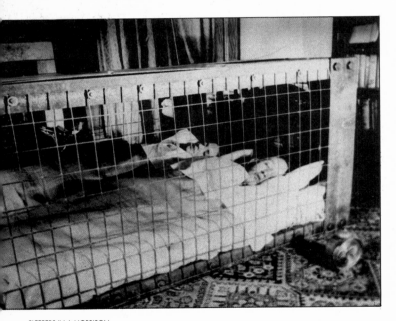

SLEEPERS IN A MORRISON SHELTER

Much of the damage to property was caused by incendiary bomb fires that were allowed to gain a hold and burn out of control. A New Year appeal was made for 10,OOO volunteer Fire Watchers. Within a month more than double that number had come forward. The scheme was that a party of six should patrol their own street or neighbourhood. Each party was issued with a stirrup pump and the individuals were promised steel helmets. A bag of sand was left at every lamp post, with 5 to 10 bags at postboxes, fire alarms and telephone kiosks, plus larger dumps in main roads and shopping centres.

At first the volunteers watched civilian premises only. The Fire Prevention (Business Premises) Order changed that, when it stated that all males between 18 and 60, working at business premises, must take turns fire watching, without pay, but not exceeding 48 hours a month. All the Fire watchers received training, reporting to fire-huts scattered around Battersea and Wandsworth. The smoke crawl was usually their first experience of being in a fire. Attired ln old clothes and boots, they had to crawl through a smoke filled room with their faces close to the floor where the air was clearer. This was followed by a lecture and practical lessons on the use of a stirrup pump and the extinguishing of an incendiary bomb. At the end of the day, the pupil would have a dry throat and a damp exterior but confident that he could cope at an incident.

These newly trained personnel were of great help over the next few months as the Germans renewed the bombing offensive, many premises being saved by the efforts of these often elderly people. One post dealt with 150 incendiaries of which not one started a major fire. At Clapham, the Stormont Road Congregational Church was hit by 5 fire-bombs, one piercing the roof, but, due to prompt action, there was no major damage.

As the bombing continued, the local authorities improved the shelter accommodation. The corridor-type shelters were constructed at first to be blast and splinter proof and then improved to withstand medium-heavy bombs. Another type was the Morrison shelter, a steel framed cage, with a solid top and open sides. They were installed inside a house and were often used as a table durlng the day. During a raid, the inhabitants crawled inside and the shelter was supposed to be strong enough to support any falling debris. Where there were no street shelters, they were provided free, but they could be purchased for £8.

In October 1940, the Ministry of Home Security decided that a comprehensive system of deep-level shelters should be built. Four sites were selected in South London along the route of the Northern Line Tube. They were at Clapham South, Clapham Common, Clapham North and Stockwell. The shelters were built between 80 and 105 feet below ground, well beyond bomb penetration, the spoil being dumped on Clapham Common. The design was of two parallel tunnels, with two levels of bunks and each could accommodate over 6,000 people, with all the modern conveniences. By the time they were finished in September 1942, the 'Blitz' was over, so they were used as hotels for the troops passing through London and later one was used as part of the D-Day preparations. It was not until the V-weapon campaign, that the deep shelters came into their own, sheltering thousands of Londoners.

The Balham Home Guard became a fully fledged battalion in March 1941, separating from the Battersea Battalion. The standing of this force had improved tremendously since its formation and had become much more professional. The Balham men had reached 'marksman' standard in rifle-shooting, winning most of the competitions against other Home Guard units. Many of the large industrial employees were also forming their own units, the Wand Gas Battalion being formed in June 1941, parading at their Worcester Park sports ground, the salute being taken by the general manager.

Some of the heaviest bombing raids occurred in the middle of April 1941. Numerous flares were dropped as well as a number of parachute mines. A heavy A.A. barrage was fired against the bombers and anyone in the open was in as much danger from nose-caps and shell splinters as from the bombs. The Alvering Library at Wandsworth was hit and virtually destroyed. Another hit was on the Castle Public House, in Putney Bridge Road. This was a new building, opened in 1939 and had been strongly built. The thick walls saved the surrounding buildings from most of the blast but the pub interior was devastated. The bars had been crowded and 42 customers were killed and 141 injured.

The bombers continued their visits the following month, with a particularly heavy raid on the 10/11th May. The bombs started to fall on the City and gradually worked westward. Atney Road and Oxford Road, Putney were badly damaged. Putney Hospital had a near miss. It had been strengthened with blast walls and steel-faced shutters but a bomb in the garden demolished the chapel and broke most of the windows in the nurses' home.

The main raids then came to a halt as the Germans became more involved in the Balkans and the Luftwaffe needed to refit in preparation for the coming attack on Russia. After a lull of seven weeks, single raiders attacked on the 27/28th July, with Central Wandsworth as the main target. Bombs were dropped on the Magdalen Road-Trinity Road-Springfield area. However, these were the last until the Spring of 1943. At last there was time to take

Members of the 52nd London (Wandsworth Gas Company) Battn. Home Guard in training. Starting with an armband for a uniform and a few rifles shared by the many as its equipment, it grew into a useful military unit.

WANDGAS HOME GUARD

stock and to catch up with repairing houses and clearing rubble. Although the resident population had fallen, the bombing had caused a housing crisis.

One of the most irritating aspects of the 'Blitz' was the black-out. It caused a large rise in road accidents and injuries to pedestrians, who tripped over kerbs or bumped into objects. How effective was the black-out? Aids to aircraft navigation were primitive at this time and thick cloud made target identification impossible. The bombers often relied on the first wave starting fires, at which the following aircraft aimed. In London, the Thames provided a familiar shape, which could not be effectively hidden.

At ground level, there were few street lights, traffic lights were not operational and vehicle headlights were masked. Many people had torches, but as they were not supposed to be used continually and then batteries became scarce, most people relied on their night vision. Moonlight and the glow from searchlights made things easier and, during air-raids, there were flares, gun flashes and the glow from fires, lighting the sky. According to a Tooting tram driver, the most difficult thing was judging distances and the size of objects. Once he stopped his tram because he thought a red light was the rear of a vehicle on the tracks. It turned out to be a glowing cigarette end!

GARRATT LANE BOMB
DAMAGE 1940/41

As the bombing came to a halt, accounts were released about the heroes and heroines of the 'Blitz'. Many people from all the different organisations received the George Medal and other awards for their bravery under fire, risking their lives to save other people. The following are just a small selection from the long list of award winners:

James Burlow was a Wandsworth Rescue Party leader. At one incident, he had rescued two youths and then crawled back under a 15 foot mound of rubble to a young girl. She was trapped by rubble and floor joists pinning her down. He managed to free her and with one hand holding back the debris he bandaged her injuries with his other hand and teeth. When he pulled her free he collapsed with exhaustion. All told he saved nine lives.

Civilian workers also did extraordinary feats, such as George Medal winner, William Holtham. He was a senior valveman at the Wandsworth Gas Works and when a gas holder was hit, he helped seal off the inlet and outlet valves. Despite being injured and suffering from concussion, as well as the extreme heat and falling debris, he continued to give instructions to prevent further explosions, only leaving for the first aid post when the task was completed.

Women too were in the thick of the action. Miss Winifred Eustace of Tooting, a driver with the Auxiliary Fire Service, was awarded the O.B.E. During a heavy raid on the docks, the roof of her mobile canteen was blown off by a bomb blast. Dazed but unhurt, she continued to drive the vehicle, dispensing well earned refreshments to the civil defence workers.

Despite the outbreak of war, the police still had to continue the peacetime duties of crime prevention and detection, as well as traffic direction, a more frequest war-time task due to blocked streets. They also had to detect and isolate delayed-action and unexploded bombs. Other duties included sounding the air-raid siren, collecting details of casualties and circulating information. On top of this, they often helped with rescue work.

At Battersea, Inspector Bates tunnelled under burning wreckage to rescue a woman and her three children for which he was awarded the George Cross. Special Constable Fred Almond crawled under a mass of overhanging debris to free a trapped man. P.C. Barry saved the South-West Magistrates Court, Lavender Hill and the official records, when incendiary bombs started a fire in the Chief Clerk's room. He managed to control the blaze, although the basement and cells were flooded.

After nearly a year of continuous bombing, the civil defence services and their personnel were exhausted and near collapse. Somehow, they fought on and with the withdrawal of the German bombers, breathed a sigh of relief, being able to get much needed time for rest and reorganisation.

WANDSWORTH HOME GUARD PARADE IN THE GROUNDS OF MAYFIELD SCHOOL

THE KITCHEN FRONT

RATIONING

At the outbreak of war, a few people who could afford it, stocked up on all sorts of tinned goods. Some items disappeared practically overnight. However, most people did not earn enough to buy in quantity and hoarding was looked upon as irresponsible.

Rationing was introduced in easy stages and ration books only came into use on Monday, 8th January 1940, for certain items. These first ration books had pages containing printed squares, which were cut out by the shop-keeper. This was a tedious and time consuming task and was changed to the squares being cancelled by a rubber stamp or indelible pencil.

The first items on ration for one person, per week, were 4 ounces of bacon or ham. 4 ounces of butter and 12 ounces of sugar. Meat rationing followed in March and was limited by price to ls 10d (7p) worth for people over 6 years and 11d (2p) worth for younger children. Offal and sausages were not rationed but the latter were very scarce and the former, such as sheep's head, were not to people's taste. On checking the Battersea area, the authorities found that not all the ration was being taken up. At first it was thought that the population figures had been over-estimated but it was found that on the whole, people were too poor to afford the full ration.

In July 1940, rationing was extended to tea, as well as margarine and cooking fats. Tea packets were torn open to get at the last grains and the authorities ran a propaganda campaign on 'None for the pot'. Butter and margarine were spread extremely thinly on bread and the wrappings scraped to remove the last vestiges of fat. The next year, the list grew to include jam, marmalade and syrup, followed by mincemeat, lemon curd and honey, collectively classified as preserves. One of the heaviest blows was when cheese was restricted to 1 ounce a week, hardly enough for a sandwich. It was soon doubled to 2 ounces a week, with agricultural workers and those doing heavy manual work receiving an extra ration. At the end of 1941, most other groceries were put on a 'points' system and it was up to the housewife how to spend her allocation. The value of items went up and down according to the availability of goods and it became like a gambling game to find items with a low points value.

Fish was not rationed but supplies were erratic. All sorts of strange types were put on sale, including something called Snook. This turned out to be whalemeat, which most people rejected as being evil-smelling and practically uneatable, however well it was disguised.

By July 1940, eggs had virtually disappeared. Thousands of chickens had been slaughtered to save on feeding stuffs. Before the war, the average

consumption was 3 eggs a week, which during the war dropped to one egg every two weeks, though there were long periods with none at all. Prices were strictly controlled and the shopkeeper had to bear the loss of any that were broken, making them unprofitable. Midway through the war, an American import appeared on the shelves – powdered egg. Although not very good in some recipes, it was a life-saver in the kitchen and the tin was equivalent to a month's family egg ration.

To help the housewife, the Wandsworth Gas Company held cookery demonstrations with the theme "Fitter though rationed". They.were shown how to make the most of both rationed meat and unrationed offal, in the form of pies, curries and stews. Sugarless puddings, simple cakes, savoury and fish dishes were also prepared. Vegetarian dishes were also prominent, with bean cutlets, enough to feed a large family, costing only 4d (less than 2p). Other dishes included vegetable pies, curried lentils and rice.

The Wandsworth Food Education Committee set up centres all over the borough to give demonstrations. A favourite was potato soup, a main course using tinned meat or a casserole for the air-raid shelter. During a class at Ensham Central School, showing how to make cakes without fat or sugar, an air-raid alert was sounded. No one bothered to go to a shelter but continued to watch the demonstration, before hurrying off to the shops to buy the necessary ingredients.

To bridge the gap between appetite and rations, a family was expected to eat out at least once a month, a meal which did not need coupons. Meals were provided for school children and all factories and businesses above a certain size were obliged by law to provide a staff canteen. The most important innovation was the British Restaurant and Feeding Centres, which provided cheap but filling meals. The first centre in our area was set up by the L.C.C.

at the Broadmede School, Clapham. It was staffed by the teachers, who had to overcome the difficulties of cooking on a field kitchen and a shortage of cutlery. A typical meal was roast lamb, baked beans and roast potatoes, followed by plum pudding and custard, washed down with a cup of tea, all for the sum of lld ($2^1/_2$p). The first British Restaurant at Putney was opened in St. Mount, a large house at 394, Upper Richmond Road.

Gradually, these cafes opened all over the area, mainly at schools or other institutions where cooking facilities were available. On their first day, Haselrigge Road School, Clapham, served 125 meals, plus 38 'take-aways'. At the Battersea Polytechnic, there were complaints about the small portions but on the whole most people were grateful for the service. One dish that was disliked by many was Woolton Pie, named after the Minister of Food, Lord Woolton. The dish was a combination of carrots, parsnips, turnips and potatoes, covered with a white sauce and topped with pastry. 'Dry and uneatable' was the general opinion and one young child, presented with his umpteenth pie of the war, took one look and burst into tears!

Vegetables were not rationed but again there could be sporadic shortages. Battersea housewives complained about the supply, They felt that hotels and big food companies were receiving priority, while rumours spread about fruit rotting on the ground. Everywhere people experimented, scrounged and made do. It became socially acceptable to stop people in the street to ask them where they obtained a particular item. A Battersea woman remembers, as a young girl, rushing off with her mother when they heard there were pieces of rabbit for sale. As there were two of them in the queue, they were able to buy two joints. Cakes were 'iced' without icing sugar and wedding cakes were just cardboard shells. Nobody went hungry but rationing was to continue long after the war.

DIGGING FOR VICTORY

A great deal of food was imported from around the world, such as the $5^1/_2$ million pounds of bacon and ham from Canada. Wheat, meat and dairy products arrived in huge quantities, all requiring a large amount of shipping space. Any food that could be produced at home meant more space for war material on the convoys. The aim was to provide half a million plots of land, which would eventually save 200,000 tons in cargo space. Wandsworth had 8,000 council houses, most with reasonable sized gardens but, as one councillor said, many had not seen a spade for years. Battersea had no official allotments but it asked the London County Council to set aside sections of Clapham Common and Battersea Park for growing crops. The commons were of rather poor soil of sand and

gravel but people made an attempt at growing produce. The lucky applicants obtained plots in the more fertile areas of the parks.

In May 1941, Double Summer Time was introduced, which put the clocks two hours in advance of G.M.T. This meant daylight lasted well into the evening, giving the farmer and amateur gardener more time to work their land. People were encouraged to concentrate on carrots, turnips and onions, although other green vegetables and root crops were permitted. Potatoes were strictly controlled, only seed potatoes being allowed for planting and not those large enough for consumption. They also had to be of disease resistant varieties.

By the end of 1940, over 4,000 plots had been provided and to encourage people, the Wandsworth

BATTERSEA PARK PIG CLUB

Pat and Mary. This enterprise was encouraged by a visit from the Minister for Agriculture and the Commissioner of the Metropolitan Police.

On the site of Winstanley School, Battersea, which had been demolished shortly before the war, a mini-farm was set up by the local A.R.P. wardens. As well as growing vegetables, they kept chickens, which gave a good supply of eggs, and several pigs. The feeding of the animals required some organising as it took several tons of feed to produce 1 ton of pork. It also took four pounds of potatoes to produce the same nutritional value as one pound of grain. Eventually, the swill buckets were left in the streets, the contents of which were well boiled and fed to the pigs.

How much produce was grown will never be known, as it was much more difficult than people thought. There were diseases, insects, rodents, drought and flood to contend with. Many hours of labour were also involved, associated with hard work and blistered hands. However, for the successful, it did provide ingredients for a more varied diet.

Council offered 30,000 spring cabbage plants for sale, at cost. Regulations were released, so that any surplus crops could be sold without a licence, as long as it was not the main means of support. Another 1,000 plots were under cultivation by July 1941, some on bomb sites. The largest allotment was in Battersea Park, being over four times the normal size. It was managed by a fireman from the Burns Road Fire Station and provided fresh vegetables for their staff canteen all year round.

Several applications were received from Council tenants to keep chickens in their back gardens and as far as possible this was allowed. The Ministry of Food also relaxed restrictions on keeping pigs but both councils were loath to allow these on private premises. However, pig clubs were encouraged and Wandsworth had the first co-operative pig club in the country. Soon they were springing up all over, in such places as Battersea Park, Wimbledon Park, King George's Park. Soon there were over twenty clubs in Wandsworth alone. To encourage others, the Council even supplied material for building pig-stys.

Organisations such as the police and air-raid posts started their own pig-clubs. One at Clapham Police Station, Union Grove, was set up on some waste ground at the rear of the building. P.C. Newham, who had been born on a farm in East Anglia, was delegated to purchase four, cross-bred, Essex pigs, which received the names Bill, Jack,

THE UNEASY CALM: MAY 1941 – MAY 1944

The war was creating difficulties with the economy, both nationally and locally. As many people had left our area, due to being called up or evacuated, the rate income had fallen, while the cost of Civil Defence had risen. Battersea decided not to build any more public air-raid shelters, as the population had declined, but was to strengthen the existing street shelters and still supply Anderson and Morrison shelters to those who required them.

Wandsworth Council was concerned about the cost of clearing the sites of demolished houses and the repair of others. Re-housing the homeless was a problem, as the housing stock was depleted by the bombing and requisitioning of property was proceeding at a slow pace. Conditions at the temporary rest centres were sometimes primitive but gradually improved. In November 1941, a 'half-way' house in Carlton Drive, Putney, was opened by the Mayor, with another in Leigham Court Road, Streatham, following shortly after. It was here that short-stay flats were provided until more permanent accommodation could be provided. Another facility being provided to bombed-out families was the mobile laundry. One was enough for 30 family washes.

Refugees were still arriving from Occupied Europe and had to be scrutinised by a counter-intelligence group at their port of entry. In April 1941, a special centre was set up at the Royal Victoria Patriotic Asylum on Wandsworth Common, under Lt. Col. Oreste Pinto, a Dutch army officer. If there was the slightest suspicion about any refugee, they were sent to Wandsworth for further investigation.

At the school there was a large room, empty of furniture, except for a long, bare table. It was nick-named the 'lumber-room', as every morning the examiners would sit at this table, with the belongings of their "clients" spread in front of them. Everything would be examined in great detail including the suitcases, wallets, fountain-pens, diaries and correspondence. At the end of the day the room looked like a cross between a customs hall and a jumble sale.

Sometimes the evidence of spying was found at this early stage, usually being materials for making invisible ink, otherwise it took hours of questioning. However long it took to unmask the spies, it was only a short journey across the road to Wandsworth Prison. By the end of 1942, 4 Germans 3 Dutch, 3 British, 2 Belgian and 1 Swiss national had been executed for being enemy agents.

Bona fide refugees were helped as much as possible. There were three hostels in Wandsworth and a number of billets. Clothing and furniture were distributed and every effort was made to find them employment, making them self-supporting, a changed attitude since the start of the war. Social clubs had been started to help the different nationals keep in contact, as well as to learn English.

Every effort was still being made to increase production and iron railings were still being removed for scrap, the total for Wandsworth being equivalent to 235 heavy tanks. There were complaints from some residents of the Tonsley Road area about the damage caused by workmen using sledge-hammers to remove the railings instead of cutting the bars. This was breaking the coping stones and concrete floors. Although the Council issued new instructions, it seemed the contractors took little notice, as the complaints still arrived. The local residents also protested about the large dumps of metal, piled up unused.

Money was being raised for all sorts of projects, by direct collection or by the sale of savings stamps and war bonds. There were schemes to adopt warships, have tanks inscribed with names, money for the Red Cross and towards armaments. Special displays and parades were a regular feature to raise money and to wave the flag. The Battersea Home Guard Battalion band was often in demand on these occasions, performing all over South London. It had expanded from its original eight members, to twenty-six, many of whom were employed by the Electricity Department of the Battersea Council.

Typical of such events was the War Weapons Week in May 1941, which included concerts, cricket matches and whist drives. The campaign was opened with a parade, the salute being taken by the local M.P., Ernest Bevin. The column stretched for a mile and included bands of the Royal Marines, the

Home Guard, the Auxiliary Fire Service and a Canadian Pipe Band. There were five floats depicting various tableaux, such as bomb disposal and salvage collection, interspersed with units from the military and many of the voluntary organisations. At Arding and Hobbs, a Messerschmitt, Me 109 fighter was on show, along with a collection of weapons, under the watchful eye of the A.T.C. Between them, the residents of Battersea and Wandsworth raised the staggering sum of just over £2 million.

In June 1941, clothes rationing was introduced, causing confusion and anger amongst the smaller retailers. Many had stocked up with wool

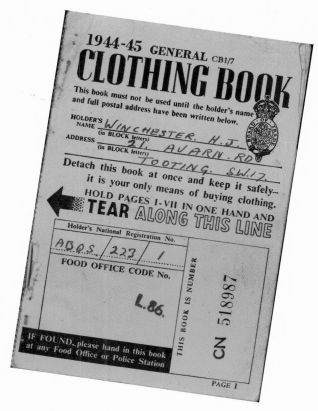

in the military colours, so that people could produce knitted items for friends or relatives in the forces. The shop-keepers were reluctant to purchase further supplies as they felt people would be reluctant to give up valuable coupons and they would be left wlth large stocks. Later in the year, the Ministry of Home Security at last gave orders

for the A.R.P. personnel to be issued with battle-dress, overcoats and boots. Another uproar occurred when the Board of Trade insisted that 18 clothing coupons be handed over in exchange. In this crazy world of bureaucracy, items such as braces and clerical and academic robes were exempt!

When people awoke on 22nd June 1941, they heard that Hitler had invaded Russia. This explained the ending of the bombing as the Luftwaffe had transferred most of its aircraft to the eastern front. At first the news was depressing, as the Germans rapidly advanced, capturing huge numbers of men and large quantities of material. However, as the months went by, the mood changed as Londoners learnt of the Russian resistance. The new allies needed supplies of all sorts but war production in Britain was still disappointingly low. Special efforts were made locally to raise money by giving concerts and organising parades.

To help increase production, young women had to register at the local labour exchange. They had to state if they were working, the type of work, previous experience, whether married, running a home and the number of their children. The idea was to fill the gaps in the munitions factories and provide volunteers for the auxiliary services. Actual conscription was introduced in December 1941, but was usually confined to unattached women between the ages of 19 and 24. Overall, the proportion called-up was very small, as most women within the group were already employed or serving in one of the voluntary services.

"ANDLE III LIMPS BACK
RT. NOVEMBER 1942

In 1939, women were already prominent in clerical work and as the war progressed, they became more noticeable on the buses and in the postal services. They also moved into industry, meeting some opposition at first but were soon doing heavy, manual work. A special school was set up at Clapham Junction Station to train women for work in the offices and on the platforms. Eventually, they manned the booking offices, the goods and parcels depots, as well as being carriage cleaners, ticket collectors and guards.

Women also cleaned buses and trams, working from 7.30am to 4.30pm, most managing six vehicles a day. Another local woman took a horse-drawn milk float out from the United Dairies depot at Balham and delivered in the Battersea area. It was physically demanding work with the loading and unloading of the cart, as well as having to look after the horse.

There were a number of important factories in the area, such as the A-1 Projectile Company at Nine Elms, making munitions. Despite the heavy bombing it escaped with minor blast damage and a dud A.A. shell that fell through the glass roof. Another major company was Morgan Crucible, situated on the riverbank next to Battersea Bridge. Their products were used in tanks, artillery, radar, searchlights, vehicles and aircraft. Over 30 items from the factory were required in the building of a Lancaster bomber. Their buildings were hit by several H.E. bombs but production was not seriously affected.

A large target at Wandsworth was the gas works but despite some damage it continued to produce gas. For this it needed a constant supply of coal, which was brought by coastal steamer from the north of England. During the First World War, one of these ships, "The Wandle", had managed to sink a U-boat, which attacked her off Sunderland. Twenty-six years later, a sister-ship the "Wandle III", was not so lucky. This vessel was attacked by E-boats on the night of 9th November, 1942 and was hit by a torpedo, sustaining considerable damage to her bows. She was saved by her captain and a volunteer, skeleton crew, who managed to sail her to Yarmouth, where temporary repairs were made.

The K.L.G. works at Putney Vale, the home of the modern spark plug, was producing vital parts for aircraft. Also involved with aircraft was the A.P.V. company at Point Pleasant, Wandsworth. They were engaged in making jettison fuel tanks, as well as developing a special fuel tank for photo-reconnaissance Spitfires. These were made from a special metal and the prototype tank required 150 separate sections. A factory was found in Garratt Lane, where six skilled men and a team of two hundred girls turned them out by the hundreds.

All over the two boroughs, small firms were producing items from uniforms to heavy equipment. Brayman's of Battersea were making tea buckets and field ovens, while James Day, sheet-metal works of Hestor Road, were constructing tank-landing craft. Fryers in Orkney Street, Battersea, were overall manufacturers, making mainly navy-blue boiler suits for the Auxiliary Fire Service. The women employees were paid piece rate,

CHANGE OF SHIFTS,
MORGANS CRUCIBLE,
BATTERSEA

each machinist working on a specific part of the garment. One of the workers, Florence Ambridge, recalls inverting sleeves on a special machine, for which she received $1\frac{1}{2}$d a pair, averaging £3 a week. The hours were 8am to 5pm, Monday to Friday and conditions were strict. However, the women were allowed to listen to "Music While You Work" and records played over the workshop tannoy. As Florence was considered a 'specialist', she was exempted from the national "call-up".

To encourage married women with children to go to work, pre-school nurseries were provided. In July, 1942, temporary huts were built by the Battersea Council in Battersea Park and on Clapham Common. Six others were already in being, three run by the Council, two by the L.C.C. and one by the Battersea Central Mission. Wandsworth had four nurseries, joined by another at Mitcham Road, Tooting in May, 1942, with two others under consideration for Streatham and Clapham. On average, these nurseries could take fifty children.

NAVAL PERSONNEL TAKE A BREAK

Although the danger had receded, the authorities were still worried about a possible invasion, preceded by a gas attack. In September, 1941, a surprise exercise was carried out at Tooting Broadway. The A.R.P. wardens sounded their wooden rattles, indicating a gas attack, which was simulated by setting off tear-gas bombs. Hundreds of people were caught without their gas masks, most being women out shopping. Road blocks were set up and only drivers with gas masks were allowed to proceed, the others being diverted. Bus passengers were advised to leave the vehicles. Unfortunate shop assistants were affected by lingering fumes long after the gas had dispersed outside.

The Home Guard units continued to train and were becoming an efficient fighting force. At dawn on Sunday, 5th October, 'enemy parachutists' landed in Battersea Park, to attack various objectives in the neighbourhood. Fire-crackers were used to simulate small-arms fire and hand grenades. Smoke bombs were extensively used by the 'enemy' to hide their movements but so effective were the Home Guard in their guerilla-war type tactics, that only one objective was reached by the 'invaders'. Similar exercises took place on Clapham and Tooting Bec Commons.

At Nine Elms, a school was set up for street-fighting, the instructors coming from the Irish Guards. The men first attended classroom lectures at the Devas Institute in Thessaly Road. They then received practical lessons in the rubble of the nearby bombed houses, learning how to deal with snipers, disarm booby-traps and how to isolate enemy patrols.

To provide refreshments to the Home Guard and other services, mobile canteens were provided, most being donated. The Mayor of Battersea took possession of one vehicle presented by the people of Kenya, which was duly handed over to the W.V.S. Another was presented by the Morgan Crucible Company, the money for which had come from a factory in Pennsylvania, which used their products. This vehicle was shared by all the services.

In Wandsworth, the Kimber family presented a canteen in memory of Sir Henry Kimber, who had been Wandsworth's M.P. between 1885 and 1913. The vehicle was based on a Ford saloon chassis, converted to a design by Cllr. Mrs Croft. It was equipped with two Calor-gas rings, two thermos cans and a copper sink. There was storage space for 120 cups, as well as food. In all, Wandsworth had a total of six vehicles, plus two trailer canteens. No doubt they were a most welcome sight during training sessions as well as at real bomb incidents.

On the 8th December 1941, the British public learnt of the attack on Pearl Harbour the previous day and that the United States were now in the war. British territory in the Far East had also been attacked and for a time things went badly for the Allies. However, it was realised that once the U.S. was geared up, the problem of supplies would become easier as time went on.

At the beginning of 1942, new Defence Regulations called for the registration of youths and girls between the ages of 16 and 18. There was no compulsion but the youngsters were encouraged to join some sort of youth organisation or to train with the Home Guard, the A.T.C. or Sea Cadets. A Girls Training Corps was formed, in which the recruits received training for the Armed Forces, nursing, munitions work or the land army. The 97th Company at Putney were soon learning how to deal with incendiary bombs. Later in the year there was compulsory registration for fire watching for men aged 18 to 59 and women 20 to 45.

There was still a deal of pressure to save both money and salvage, especially paper. Pressed paper was used for a great variety of military purposes, especially in aircraft. It was used for long-range fuel tanks and navigation tables. Wadding in bullets came from waste paper. The rear, four-gun turret of a Lancaster bomber fired 5,000 rounds a minute, which used the equivalent of 4 1b envelopes every five seconds.

Even a new issue of ration books consumed 7,000 tons of paper. During a special salvage drive, Wandsworth aimed to win a prize for the largest amount collected.

The 21st-28th March, 1942 was declared Warship Week and the usual parade and concerts were organised. The idea was that if a target for fund raising was reached, the borough could 'adopt'

H.M.S. BULLDOG
Imperial War Museum

a warship. Wandsworth collected £1$^3/_4$ million and chose the anti-aircraft cruiser, H.M.S. Cairo. Unfortunately before a presentation plaque could be fixed to the ship, it was sunk. It was on a Malta convoy and had already fought off several air attacks when it was hit by a torpedo. Fortunately, there were few casualties. The Streatham Auxiliary Fire Service men made a large scale model of the ship, in their spare time, which they pulled through the streets to raise money. The following year, a bronze replica of the ship's badge was presented to the borough, as a memorial and tribute to the crew.

Battersea raised £$^1/_2$ million and adopted a destroyer, H.M.S. Bulldog. It turned out to be a 'lucky' ship, surviving many operations. It had taken part in the rescue of H.M.S. Kelly; survived bombings at Dunkirk and the Norway campaign; been on convoys to Russia; took part in the later North Africa landings and acted as escort to transports in the Mediterranean and the Pacific. Here too

was an exchange of badges.

The war news was not good, as U-boats continued to take a heavy toll of shipping. Rommel had taken Tobruk and was advancing on Alexandria. There was great pressure to produce more armaments and provide more men at the front. In Battersea Park, the A.A. batteries were manned by volunteers from the Battersea Home Guard and the barrage balloon units were taken over by W.A.A.F.s, so releasing regular soldiers for duty overseas.

The constant pressure for more production was having an effect with absenteeism beginning to rise. Management and working methods were often old-fashioned and many of the practices irritated the workforce. The only time output went up occurred during 'Russian' week, when all that week's production went to help the Soviets. Many of the workers admired the Russians because of the stand made by the Red Army against the Germans and the apparent strength of the 'worker state'. The Government, uneasy about the unrest, took over the

H.M.S. CAIRO PRESENTATION
PLAQUE 1942

more important factories and gave the workforce more of a direct say about how it was to be run.

The authorities recognised the importance of leisure and midday concerts were often arranged in canteens. Outside the work place there were dance halls, such as the Streatham Locarno, where you could dance the night away. During the summer, a special campaign was started to encourage 'stay-at-home' holidays. The London County Council organised an extensive.programme where there was a choice of a number of open-air entertainments from variety shows to Shakespeare.

Every open space, such as Clapham Common had its fair or fete, although one side-show missing was the coconut shy. At King George's Park, athletics meetings were held as well as providing many other sporting facilities. Open-air dances were popular and schools were kept open so children could play under supervision. Cycling was popular, as there were virtually no private cars and public transport was crowded. This, however, led to an enormous increase of bicycle thefts.

At last, things started to improve. Production started to rise in the factories, enabling the 8th Army in North Africa to have four times as many tanks as the Germans, leading to the victory at El Alamein. The Home Intelligence secret reports noted that most people in London wanted a swift end to the war, with a 'second front' opened in France. Churchill insisted on a more long term view and that the North African campaign had to be

finished first. The war was to last a lot longer and people had to be persuaded to keep working flat out. The year 1943 followed much the same pattern as before, with parades, and displays exercised by the Home Guard. The Wandsworth Battalion held a demonstration of its capabilities on Wimbledon Common. Signallers, pioners, despatch riders, A.A. gunners, telephonists, clerks all showed off their specialities, while the combat troops gave displays of armed and unarmed combat and physical training.

The Air Training Corps was now well established with a squadron for each of the Parliamentary divisions. At Putney, No. 1352 Squadron moved into new headquarters at 65 Upper Richmond Road, where there were large classrooms and mess facilities. Putney also had a Women's Junior Air Corp, which trained girls between the ages of 14 and 18, for entry into the W.A.A.F or the other services. The 34F Squadron of Balham and Tooting received a surprise visit from King Haaken of Norway and the Crown Prince. The squadron, based at Fircroft School and winners of a proficency test cup, put on a display of drill and counter-marching.

The main savings campaign for 1943 was "Wings for Victory". A four engined bomber cost about £40,000 and a typical bomb load £5,500. The Putney area managed to raise nearly £18,000. There was also a campaign against wasting bread. This was not rationed but the wheat had to be shipped from North America and the U-boat menace was still high. Water was another target, with an average household using 5 tons a week. By reducing this by a fifth, there would be a large saving on coal and electricity, capacity which could be switched to war production. In the salvage drive, bones were highlighted. When processed, bones yielded nitroglycerine, lubricating oils, glue, foodstuffs for pigs and hens and fertiliser.

The beginning of 1943 also saw the first concentrated raids on London since the 'Blitz'. These were in retaliation for heavy Allied attacks on Berlin. Christchurch Road, Streatham was hit and the other end of Wandsworth received attention as well. On the evening of 3rd March, 1941, numerous incendiaries had been dropped and a parachute flare drifted towards Putney. The following bombs landed in Dryburgh, Egliston and Erpingham Roads, fracturing a gas main which caught fire, burning for many hours.

Battersea too received attention. On the night of 17th/18th January, two raids had high explosive bombs falling in Albert Bridge Road, Battersea Park and Nine Elms. In March, it was the turn of South Battersea, this time mainly an incendiary attack, with canisters falling in the Wakehurst Road and Bramfield Road area. Casualties were also caused by faulty A.A. shells which exploded only after falling back to the ground.

ANGLO-SOVIET MEETING, BATTERSEA PARK, 1941

The British defences had substantially improved with radar equipped fighters and new A.A. rocket projectors and all were more successful. The Luftwaffe gave up after these two raids but hit and run night raids still took place during October and November. Battersea again took all the hits, except one. One major incident occurred on the 20th November, when a large H.E. bomb landed in the middle of Beaufoy Road, 40 yards from the junction of Eversley Road, causing extensive blast damage and fracturing the water and gas mains. An off-licence and a dairy-shop were extensively damaged and great care was taken to salvage as much of the stock as possible. There were 8 fatalities, 41 people needing hospital treatment and a further 50 needed shelter, which was provided at the Basnett Road School.

Such widespread damage was caused because some bombs were fitted with a long tube on the nose, causing it to explode just above ground level. This was the case in the incident which occurred on the evening of the 7th November, 1943, at Putney. People were leaving the two cinemas in the High Street and queues were forming at the bus stops. Suddenly, a single plane swooped low, releasing a 500 kilo bomb. This hit the Black and White Milk Bar at the corner of Putney Bridge Road, exploding on contact. On the upper floor was a dance hall crowded with young people enjoying a Sunday night's entertainment.

The upper floor collapsed onto the ground floor milk bar, where there were about thirty customers. Miraculously, some received only cuts and bruises, while others were crushed by slabs of concrete. Rubble was strewn across the road and a furniture store opposite had its stock reduced to matchwood. Flying glass caused many injuries. The rescue services soon arrived and an incident post was set up in the wreckage of an optician's. The foyer of the Palace Cinema was used as a first aid station before the injured were taken off to the neighbouring hospitals.

Then came the grim task of recovering the dead and injured from the heaped ruins. Some were lucky, escaping virtually unscathed, while others, who looked like they were unconscious, had been killed by the blast. Identification of the living and the dead was difficult, especially in the case of women, who had become separated from their handbags containing their documents. It was weeks before some were reunited with relatives, as nobody knew to which hospital they had gone. A crane was brought in to remove the larger blocks of masonry and concrete and by the next day enough of the debris had been cleared to allow the trolleybuses to inch their way past the wreckage. The final toll of casualties was 18 killed and 210 injured.

AWAITING NEWS OF FRIENDS

DERELLA' DANCE HALL,
IEY. BOMBED 7th
EMBER 1942

By the end of 1943, people began to realise that all the sacrifices and efforts were at last taking effect. The Germans and Italians had been pushed out of North Africa and landings had taken place on Sicily and the Italian mainland. In Eastern Europe, the Red Army was on the offensive and the Japanese expansion stopped. Serious planning for the invasion of Northern Europe could now begin.

On the Home Front, regulations concerning clothing were relaxed a little. From the 1st February, everyone was to receive 24 extra clothing coupons. Men were allowed to order double-breasted suits and the trousers could have turn-ups once again. To boost individual production, it was decided that London's industrial capacity was to be used to the full, now that the threat of heavy aerial bombardment had receded.

This optimism was a little premature, as, during February and March 1944, the Luftwaffe attacked in strength, in what became known as the "Little Blitz". The pattern was of fairly short alerts, distant explosions, heavy gunfire and German planes overhead. Putney received more attention than other areas. A typical raid took place in the early hours of Saturday, 19th February 1944, which lasted for $1^1/_4$ hours. Among the bombs dropped were over 100 incendiary containers, each holding 620 bombs. They fell over a wide area but fortunately they were of the non-explosive type. The contents of one container dropped along the length of Hazlewell Road and several houses were gutted by fire. Mayfield School and Whitelands College on West Hill were damaged and the District Line between East Putney and Southfields was closed because of an unexploded bomb in Sutherland Grove.

The next evening was the turn of Battersea and Wandsworth, over 150 bombs falling in one hour. These were a mixture of high explosives, phospherous-oil and incendiary bombs. Some of the latter, which did not ignite, were found to contain sand, the work of some brave, forced-labourer in Germany. One large bomb fell at the Clapham Junction end of Falcon Road, causing extensive damage to overhead wires and the tram lines, putting the service out of commission for nearly three months.

The rescue services coped very well, having been joined by the Home Guard. During 1943, they had received training in civil defence, now that a German invasion was highly unlikely. At any particular incident, they placed themselves under the incident officer, working under his supervision. The Fire-Guard also proved very effective, with 75% of the incendiary bombs being put out without the aid of the fire services.

These bombs now had to be approached with caution, as the Germans had incorporated anti-personnel devices. The fire-fighter had to approach, wriggling on his stomach, while holding some sort of shield, like a dustbin lid, in front of him. He then had to try to lob enough sand onto the incendiary to put it out.

One cause of concern to the Fire Service was the amount of rubbish being thrown into the emergency, static water tanks, which were dotted about the two boroughs. One tank in Rookstone Road, Tooting, contained over 120 milk bottles, which at first was blamed on schoolboys. However, another in Garratt Lane, near the Broadway, was found to be nearly filled with rubble, including a dustbin and parts of a kitchen range.

As the year progressed, daily life became less hectic and although there were air-raid alerts through to April 1944, no bombs fell on Battersea or Wandsworth. The year's big parade was held in March, with this year's theme being on the army, and was called "Salute the Soldier". The Wandsworth parade started from King George's Park, led by the band of R.A.F. Fighter Command. The column was made up of detachments from the U.S. forces, the searchlight batteries, the Home Guard, the A.T.S. and the various cadet forces. Static displays were also arranged in the windows of a local store and at Wandsworth Town Hall. These included aircraft petrol tanks, artillery pieces, bomb racks and parts of searchlights. Nearly £2 million was raised in National Savings, bringing Wandsworth's total since the outbreak of the war to £22 million.

At Battersea, the parade formed up in Battersea Park and included units from the Americans, the Free French and the Polish forces. The columns made a circuitous route through the local streets and ended up at 'Speakers Corner' on Clapham Common. Other parades were held in Clapham and from Balham to Tooting. The former aimed to raise £120,000, enough to pay for eight medium tanks.

On the Home Front, both councils were desperately trying to repair as many houses as possible. Since September 1940, Battersea had had 1,600 houses demolished, over 600 severely damaged and another 19,000 with less serious damage. Wandsworth also had comparable damage. A great effort was being made on making temporary repairs so that people could move back into their homes. The Government had agreed to pay £500 per house and £400 per flat, so that overcrowding could be relieved and rent income collected.

Progress was being made by the local authorities, although there were shortages of skilled labour and materials, such as plasterboard, slates and glass. Businesses were being helped as well. The Clapham Chamber of Commerce set up a scheme where all its members would help owners of small businesses affected by the bombing, to set up temporary premises, so that they could carry on trading. However, within weeks much of the work was undone, when a new, more menacing bombing campaign took place.

V–BOMBS AND VICTORY

The Allied Command had made a decision for a seaborne invasion of northern France in August 1943, but preparations were to be thorough and there was to be no early attack. By the beginning of 1944, the plans were well advanced, perhaps some of them being made at Putney, where General Eisenhower was said to have had one of his headquarters. It was a race against time as the Allies knew about Hitler's new weapons, which could destroy the invasion before it began. The building of the huge concrete caissons for the floating harbours was proving difficult and much of the work was transferred to dockyards along the lower Thames. A tremendous shortage of labour was developing in London and many of the workers were taken away from local housing repairs.

These preparations were kept secret but it became obvious that the 'Invasion' was soon to take place. Men and material began to flow through London and there was a build up of military camps and depots all over Southern England. A strip ten miles deep all around the coast, from the Wash to Land's End, was forbidden to the general public.

Locally, the Home Guard had taken over the manning of some A.A. batteries completely, releasing the regular soldiers for the coming battle.

In the early hours of Tuesday, 6th June 1944, the Allies made their landings on the Normandy beaches. As the news was released that a secure foothold had been established, the tension and pressure of the last few months now diminished. Surprisingly, little appeared in the local papers, probably because the news was being thoroughly reported by the national 'dailies'. With good news filling the papers, the public little suspected what was in store for them.

On Tuesday, 13th June, 1944, just as it was getting light, a strange noise was heard above London. It was described as sounding like an old motor-cycle, a motor-mower or a buzz-saw. The noise suddenly stopped, to be followed a few seconds later by a large explosion. The first V-1 flying bomb had arrived, exploding in Bow, East London.

The authorities had known of its existence for some time and bombing raids on the research facilities at Peenemunde and other sites had delayed.

V-1 BLAST DAMAGE TO BATTERSEA FACTORY 1944

production. There had also been delays caused by technical problems and inter-service rivalry. The Allied airforces had attacked launching sites, factories and chemical works, putting back the start of the bombardment until after the invasion of France had taken place.

On that first day, ten missiles were launched, only one reaching London. Even so, it had had a devastating effect. To avoid any panic by the public, Herbert Morrison, the Minister of Home Security, censored any reference to this new menace. When the intensity of the attacks increased, it was impossible to conceal what was happening. It was announced that London was under attack from pilotless planes but the true nature of the weapon and its destructive power was still not revealed.

The Fieseler Fi.103 or V-l, was a very efficient weapon and economical to produce but was only effective against large targets, such as cities, pin-point aiming not being possible. The bomb was just over 25 feet long, had a wing-span of 16 feet and carried a war-head of about 1 ton of high explosive. It was launched from a catapult, crossed the Channel at about 340 m.p.h., reaching a top speed of about 400 m.p.h. over England, at a height of 2-3,000 feet.

The V-ls size and speed made it extremely difficult to intercept or shoot down. Over half the A.A. guns had been withdrawn from London and now the defences had to be re-established quickly. Fighters over the Channel were the first line of defence and then a solid line of A.A. guns along the coast. More fighters covered Sussex and Kent, while all along the North Downs were hundreds of barrage balloons, rapidly brought from all over the country. Further A.A. guns were sited in the suburbs but it was found that unless the V-ls exploded in the air, they still caused great damage when they crashed to the ground.

GUARDING THE REMAINS OF A V-1, STREATHAM, 1944

The next day, the 14th June, the noise of more "doodlebugs" could be heard, which became a deep booming note as it approached, turning into a rattle from the pulse jet as it went overhead. At night you could see a flame flaring from the exhaust pipe, varying in colour from white to a deep red. It was not until the 17th June that the first bombs came to earth in our area. About 2am, the now familiar sound was heard approaching Streatham. The engine stopped and the bomb dived into the old Empire Cinema and a sheet of flame shot skywards, as debris, glass and tiles crashed all around.

The cinema was in use as an emergency food store, stacked high with tons of tea, sugar and tinned foodstuffs of all kinds. The firemen had to clamber up tottering mountains of tins and packing cases, helped by wardens, trying to pierce the smoke with their torches, as well as holding fire-hoses. There were few casualties, one being the caretaker who had been inside the cinema when the bomb hit but escaped with only shock and a few bruises. A nearby resident, in bed at the time, heard a warden climbing the stairs calling out for everyone to stay where they were. This was good advice, as his torch revealed the floor littered with glass, very menacing to bare feet!

The neighbouring railway line was blocked by debris but this was soon cleared and trains ran normally. Lineswomen from the Post Office arrived, climbing the telephone poles with great skill, soon having the lines reconnected. A number of shops were wrecked and had to be guarded from looters. Much of the food from the shops and the cinema was saved and soon taken away to other storage. Pieces of battered metal were found, complete with German lettering. These were remains of the V-l and were soon whisked away by R.A.F. intelligence to glean as much information from the wreckage as possible.

Later that afternoon, the Battersea police reported the explosion of a glider plane on St. John's Hill, Clapham Junction. It landed in the road badly damaging the Surrey Hounds public house, partly demolished a row of shops and wrecked two passing trolley-buses, causing heavy casualties. The effects were felt over a wide area, the blocked-road causing major traffic diversions.

The initiative clearly lay with the Germans and a constant stream of flying-bombs droned their way to London. Already the southern suburbs, especially Battersea, Wandsworth and Croydon, were being badly damaged. Streatham was to take the worst of the damage in Wandsworth, with a total of 41 bombs out of the 122 that fell on the borough. On the morning of Sunday, 18th June, three bombs arrived within a twenty-five minute period but mercifully casualties were light. However, the damage was enormous, later figures showing that 3,000 properties had been affected, one bomb alone accounting for 1,671 buildings. Many of the houses that remained habitable lacked gas and electricity, so that the L.C.C. had to open an emergency meals service at a nearby hall.

Battersea also received three hits that day. The first occurred at 5.30am, when three people died, the next at 8.45am, which exploded in the Battersea Rise cemetry and the last and most serious at just after midday, which struck Tennyson Street on the Shaftesbury Park Estate. The Battersea Control received a message, which simply said, "Casualties, big incident". This was no exaggeration, as the final casualties were 19 dead, 35 seriously injured and 84 slightly hurt.

IT ST JOHN'S HILL,
EA 14th JUNE 1944
fo

About two hours earlier, another disasterous incident happened at Putney. It was officially described as "a direct hit on shop premises in the Upper Richmond Road at the junction with Charlwood Road, causing the collapse of several shops and major damage to house property on the north side of the railway and the temporary blockage of the permanent way by debris".

Mr. Geoffrey Haines, deputy district warden and bomb recognition officer wrote how he approached the incident from the High Street. "As I turned into the Upper Richmond Road, a cloud of smoke and dust was slowly moving towards the car. As we went carefully onwards the cloud became so dense that we nearly ran into a bus, lying on its side, with no sign of the driver, conductor or passengers. Avoiding the debris we crawled to halt near Warden Post B8."

This post was built into the basement of premises on the other corner of Quill Bridge, which had been badly damaged. Owing to its sheltered position, no casualties had occurred amongst the wardens, though they emerged rather dazed. Mr Haines continues: "The smoke and dust were now clearing and it was possible to see that the damage was widespread and serious and that there must be a number of casualties. At nearly every window of a block of flats on the eastern corner of the bridge, people were leaning out, shouting for help, as the rear of the building had been destroyed by blast and a fire had started in the shops beneath. The four railway tracks were covered in debris and some houses north of the railway had been blown to pieces. The roof of the nearby Methodist church had been lifted several inches by the blast and then dropped back into place, while the police station had all its windows broken."

An Incident headquarters was needed and two sitting rooms of the Christian Scientist church in Gwendolen Avenue were commandeered. The Fire Brigade arrived and it took a number of engines several hours to get the blaze under control.

FLATS AT QUILL BRIDGE,
PUTNEY. HIT ON THE
18th JUNE, 1944

The heavy and light rescue services helped rescue those marooned in the flats, to be ferried away by ambulances and firstaid cars. Mortuary vans, cranes and bulldozers were asked for and quickly sent, with valuable help given by the Home Guard and the Royal Engineers. Over 300 people were involved at one time or another. The front of the flats was in a dangerous condition and a few days later was demolished by a squad of sappers. It was some time before the total casualties were known, as a number of people were unaccounted for at first. The final figures were 3 killed, 15 seriously hurt and another 10 with slight injured.

The renewed bombing brought renewed suffering, just as a wave of optimism had been created by the D-Day landings. Although under half of the V-ls launched were reaching London, between the 14th June and the end of August, there had been 407 alerts, with only one day without an explosion occurring locally. People began to look haggard through lack of sleep, as the V-ls came day and night, in rain or shine. People became paranoid, thinking that a bomb had picked them out of a crowd and you could hear them muttering, "go on, go on", wishing the engine not to cut out over them.

Some thought that the bombs were 'intelligent' or specially guided, as some categories of buildings seemed to be hit more than others, such as schools, churches and hospitals. Putney Hospital, St. James' and Bolingbroke Hospitals all had narrow escapes. Most were tall buildings, standing above the surrounding houses and so often caught the effect of blast from nearby bombs.

Transport was also badly affected. Battersea bus garage was damaged three times in two weeks and the tram depot at Clapham received a direct hit. Buses, trams and trolleybuses out on their routes, were caught in various incidents. At Battersea, a V-l hit a lorry on Lavender Hill, where the entrance to the Gateway supermarket now stands, killing 14 people in the street and the surrounding buildings. Another 14 died, passengers on a number 77 bus that was passing at the time.

The deep shelters built along the northern line came into their own. The entrances to the one at Clapham were named after various poets. Some people began to spend nearly all their time under ground and officials feared that a 'deep shelter mentality' would develop. The war was nearly over

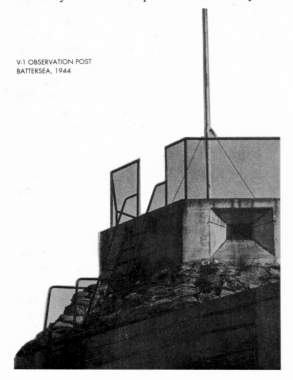

V-1 OBSERVATION POST
BATTERSEA, 1944

and no-one wanted to be killed at this late stage of the war. Others were evacuated, either under their own steam or by the local authorities. Some Battersea schoolchildren were sent to Leicester and others to Devon. Five boys, not liking their new surroundings, decided to walk home but only managed 40 miles before being discovered.

The old air-raid warning system was unable to cope as the V-ls were coming over about every 20 minutes and, being small, evaded the radar system. Often there was no warning of the arrival of the bomb and many people were caught out in the street. The constant bombardment was also having an effect on industrial production. Some of the local workforce had lost their homes, while others found the public transport system badly disrupted. Some factories, with high vantage points, had spotters permanently on look-out. When they saw a V-1 approaching, coming in their direction, an amber warning was given, followed by a red alert, when it was clear that the bomb was heading directly towards the building. This cut down the amount of stoppage time in a factory, with some workers literally diving under their workbenches at the last moment or squeezing into a two-man, reinforced steel shell, not much bigger than a pillar box.

Morgan Crucible at Battersea had such a system and were fortunate not to receive any direct hits, although there was blast damage from near misses. One bomb fell on barges moored in the river. The neighbouring factories of 'Gartons' and 'Prices' were not so fortunate and were damaged. On the 15th July, 1944, a V-1 glided down into the glucose works, followed a few minutes later by another that hit the candle factory. The latter hit the boiler house setting fire to the fuel oil. This spewed into the Thames, burning barges moored at their wharf. It took 25 fire appliances to control the fire and when the boiler house was finally pumped dry, it was found that two of the engineers had been killed.

The same day, the Nine Elms Gas Works was also badly damaged. The Secretary of State for Air witnessed the event, commenting: "Thick black clouds of dust hid it from our view and then a sheet of flame shot up." The V-1 had hit some retort chambers nearly 100 yards from the gasholders but the blast had set the gasholder ablaze.

Look outs were also posted at firestations, whose hose drying towers provided excellent vantage points. At Streatham, the station was built on high ground and from the top of the fifty foot tower you could see for several miles. At first, a large oak tree and a church steeple were in direct line with the usual approach of the V-ls but both obstacles were soon removed. When the 'Doodlebug' crashed, the look out would report "due South-East, one mile", and within seconds the rescue appliances would be on their way.

BARGES ABLAZE AT
BATTERSEA. 13th JULY 1944

One such time, the target was Freshwater Road on the Furzedown Estate. The Fire service flying squad and nearby wardens were soon on the scene, forming human chains to remove the debris in search of the injured. Hardly had the site been cleared when another flying bomb appeared and the engine cut out. Everybody dived for cover amongst the rubble. There was a terrific roar, followed by the crashing of falling houses, with the whole area enveloped in a choking cloud of dust and smoke. The bomb had fallen only 150 yards away in Welham Road, near the junction with Rectory Lane. The blast had affected the whole area, including St. Benedict's Hospital, where five wards were damaged.

Ensham School in Franciscan Road had a close call. One morning, horrified watchers saw a V-1 fall towards the school. It missed and landed in Eswyn Road. Rescuers rushed to the school but fortunately nobody was hurt. A small boy standing amongst the debris, clutching a prized piece of the V-1, said, "We didn't hear it coming but we heard the bang and all the windows came out." He then went off to join his friends in search of more metal fragments, the usual pastime of boys in those days.

As August progressed, the number of bombs declined as the launching sites in France and Belgium were over run. Some V-1s were launched from Heinkel bombers but these arrived all along the East Coast and not specifically at London. The last V-1 on our locality fell near Highlands Heath, a block of flats on Putney Heath. Arding and Hobbs, the department store at Clapham Junction, placed an advert in the South London Press, stating

"We are happy to report that nothing has occurred to prevent our giving our usual efficient and courteous service in all departments".

Wandsworth was the hardest hit of all the London boroughs during the eleven week period, with 124 bombs crashing within its boundaries, Streatham suffering the greatest damage. Although Battersea had only 36 hits, the damage per acre was greater.

At the beginning of September 1944, rumours spread that the bombing was all over and the official evacuation of London was ended. Many considered that the war was virtually over and many families returned to the capital. This relaxation was premature as on the evening of the 8th September, a mysterious explosion was heard all over London, from the Chiswick district. The government ordered a total censorship on the true cause, putting out the story that there had been a gas leak.

Other explosions followed, so that by the end of October it was clear that it was a new bombing campaign. The V-2 rocket was now in use. No warning of their arrival was possible, as the rockets travelled faster than the speed of sound, reaching their target in four minutes. The first anyone knew of the rocket's arrival was a double bang, so loud that even ten miles away it sounded close. This was followed by a reddish flash and a large column of black smoke rose skyward. At the point of impact there would be a crater as much as fifty feet across and ten feet deep. In the immediate vicinity whole rows of houses would be completely flattened.

There was no official announcement until the 10th November, more than two months after the first explosion. The first of the seven rockets had landed in Wandsworth only four days previously. Fortunately, this one landed in the middle of Tooting Bec Common, near the Avenue, making a large crater and shaking the surrounding houses. On Sunday, 19th November, another fell in Hazelhurst Road, Tooting, reducing many houses to rubble, killing 35 people and injuring another 106.

Battersea was only affected by one rocket in January 1945, which hit at the boundary with Wandsworth. It demolished many houses in Petergate, near the junction with York Road. Bulldozers were called for and again it was found that there were heavy casualties. Two others came down on Clapham one demolishing the tram depot and the last, in March 1945, came down in Tooting.

was set up at Sellincourt School, even though this was badly damaged. All the services were represented under the direct control of the Town Clerk, Major Jerman, and over 4,600 enquiries were dealt with. One disheartening aspect was that the council had only just finished repairing the houses, so all the work had come to nothing.

Earlier in the year, the authorities had been able to cope with the housing problem, as they had been steadily making houses habitable again, plus many people had left at the start of the V-bomb 'blitz'. Although not so heavy a tonnage of explosives were dropped as in 1940-41, much more blast damage was caused, often affecting over 1,000 properties at one time. It became a common sight to see windows boarded up and roofs draped with tarpaulin, weighed down with sandbags.

Wandsworth had to deal with 7,000 house-

V-2 ROCKET INCIDENT, PETERGATE, WANDSWORTH 1944

On Tuesday, 6th March, the children of 'Nutwell Street were having their lunch, when the V-2 crashed into a previously blitzed site, demolishing some prefabs and nearby flats, not only in Nutwell Street but also in Sellincourt Road. It was pitiful to see the school children lying about, badly cut and bleeding. Many people rushed to help and the Rev. R. Neill, the Rector of Tooting, drove up with his daughter, their car loaded with cups and saucers, and began to provide tea for victims and rescuers alike.

As elsewhere, during the bombings of the last few months, an Emergency Information Centre

holds moving, 60% having to put their surviving furniture into store. Nobody knew if their house would be there when they returned from work, as illustrated by the experience of a Clapham resident.

"I knew there was something wrong as soon as I came out of the tube station, as there was broken glass everywhere. My road, Downer's Cottages, was just off the main road and as I approached I felt in my pocket for my front door key. When I turned the corner, I found the entire street of ten houses had gone. There was just a huge mess of rubble, chunks of broken brickwork and tangled roof timbers."

Fortunately, it appears no one was hurt in this incident and he was reunited with his family at a rest centre in Bonneville Road School.

Battersea had lost over 2,300 houses completely and Wandsworth over 4,100. Those needing some sort of repair were 30,000 and 72,000 respectively, meaning that virtually every domestic premises in both boroughs needed some sort of attention. The South London Press reported on a visit to the office of the Battersea Borough Engineer, where the reporter saw a map covered with different coloured pins. Forty-eight contractors were at work, employing some 1,500 men, who managed to make most of the damaged houses weatherproof before the onset of winter.

Work was often held up by the shortage of materials. A press report said that in Battersea, Wandsworth and Lambeth alone, over 9 million square feet of glass was needed, enough to cover Clapham Common. Craftsmen were in short supply, with roofers only being able to cope with 450 homes a week, Battersea having 15,000 awaiting attention. During the V-1 bombing, one householder would find his workmen suddenly taken away, as they dashed off to a recent incident. Workers were recruited from other parts of Britain and from Eire but many only stayed for a short while, put off by the continuous bombardment.

The local councils were not helped by government 'red-tape'.

In theory the system was simple, with the local authority reclaiming the cost of building works from the War Damage Commission. Repairs up to £10 were undertaken without prior authority and those up to £100 were approved automatically. Above this amount, a building licence was required, which caused much criticism of civil servants sticking doggedly to the rules, even if only a few pounds were required to finish the work. It seemed they would rather someone go homeless than cause the Government extra cost.

There was also an outcry about how some places obtained a building permit. Residents of some small cottages in Garratt Lane were amazed to see the neighbouring Wandsworth Stadium being quickly re-roofed, while their own homes were open to the weather. They were told that there was valuable Tote machinery that would go rusty if not sheltered, which incensed a nearby factory manager, who had valuable machinery for making prefabricated houses. He was still waiting for his repair permit!

Prefabricated dwellings had been one of the answers to the housing problem, the Portal model being the main type, consisting of five rooms. These used a great deal of scarce materials and the Wandsworth Council favoured the more economical Uni-Seco type. There was also a Nissen-hut structure on a concrete base. Canada had sent examples of designs based on either aluminium, beaver board or plywood.

Some of the first Portal type had been erected in Blackshaw Road, Tooting, with the rent set at 10 shillings (50p) a week, with another 1 shilling and 10 pence (9p) to cover gas and electricity costs. Even this essential work did not go smoothly. Wandsworth had asked for 300 units and Battersea 750. At first the authorities dragged their feet, preferring permanent house building to have priority. Eventually they received a first batch of 115 units.

The local councils had thought that they would be in charge of the re-housing programme but the London County Council announced that they would compulsorily take over small bomb sites and erect pre-fabs which were to last for ten years. There was an outcry from the home owners as many had planned to rebuild for themselves. After pressure

PRE-FAB, STERNHOLD AVENUE, STREATHAM

from the local councils, it was decided to erect the majority of the new pre-fabs around the edges of the various commons. Despite the rebuilding campaign and the requisitioning of houses, Wandsworth still had 1,795 families waiting for a home.

As the Allies pushed the Germans back, it became obvious that the threat of a Nazi invasion was finally past. Arrangements were made for the Home Guard units to be disbanded, starting with those in the north. Fortunately, the local battalions were still up to strength during the V-bomb period and proved a tremendous help in rescuing people from the rubble of their homes. They also provided sentries against looters, who once again had become a menace. These people were often appearing during the day, posing as officials or 'volunteers', tidying up a bomb site. During October 1944, the bombing rapidly diminished so that on the 1st November, the Home Guard units were officially told to "stand-down", although some would still be held in reserve. Each battalion held its final parade, with the Mayor of Wandsworth taking the salute of a march past, outside the Municipal Buildings.

In September, the black-out restrictions had been eased and people were allowed to use ordinary curtains on their windows once more. Street lighting was switched on but only at 'night-light' strength. To help those who had lost their homes, Wandsworth was adopted by Bristol and the West Country, who sent spare furniture. This was distributed by the W.V.S. to those in need.

Despite the good news on the military front, the civilian population was becoming war weary. Absenteeism from work had become a major problem and thousands of hours were lost in factories and at the office. During the times of crisis, workers and management had co-operated but from late 1942, strikes had become more frequent. These were illegal and strikers could be imprisoned, with the press extremely hostile to any stoppages. Both sides were manoeuvering for a strong bargaining position for when the war ended.

The housewife was also finding daily life more difficult. Rationing was still strictly controlled and people were fed-up with trying to invent new recipes for using carrots and turnips. Women queued for hours to obtain ingredients for a wholesome meal. Butchers were treated as long lost friend on the off chance that you would have the privilege of receiving an extra sausage or perhaps some pig's trotters. A mother would 'kill' for fresh fruit but most children did not know what a banana looked like or how it was peeled.

The rationing of clothing was also hitting living standards. In 1942, the basic allowance was small but the real effect was only just becoming apparent, as clothes were beginning to wear out. The 'Make do and Mend' campaign and better 'utility' clothes had helped but even so most people began to look shabby. Young women especially felt the shortages. Some resorted to dyeing their legs with gravy browning and then getting a friend to pencil a seam down the back to imitate nylon stockings, which were a long vanished luxury.

Everyday items such as toothbrushes and paste, razor blades and even toilet paper became extremely scarce. Millions of pieces of crockery had been smashed and some families were reduced to drinking out of jam jars. Cutlery was almost impossible to replace and restaurants and cafes lost huge quantities through pilfering, leading to the teaspoon being attached by string to the counter for stirring tea. One item not in short supply was coal, as the emergency dumps had been stocked up throughout the two boroughs. Although there was a limited allocation per person, most people had enough to see them through the cold of January and February, 1945.

People were crying out for the necessities of life, which led to a large increase in crime, a fifty percent rise over the 1938 figures. Much went unrecorded because of the reduced police force and the black-out conditions. Most of the crime increase was accounted for by the 'black market' as the demand for everyday, rationed items grew. Lorries were hijacked and warehouses ransacked. People with the opportunity pilfered from their place of work. Clothing coupons could be bought and under the counter deals made in shops. There was a wide-spread belief that the rich were finding ways around the rationing and the Communist Party began to attract more support, especially in the poorer areas.

In March 1945, the last V-2 fell on London and the election became the main talking point. Ernest Bevin announced that he would be standing again for Wandsworth. His main opponent was to be Brigadier General J.G. Smyth, V.C., M.C. Politics were forgotten for a few days when, on Monday 7th April, the surrender of Germany was announced and the following day was declared V.E. (Victory-Empire) Day. Magically, flags, buntings and other decorations appeared, festooning streets and houses. The Wandsworth Town Hall was floodlit and at the open-air dance on Clapham Common, the searchlight battery provided a backdrop of brilliant, weaving lights. Bonfires were built on open spaces and even in the roads.

There were also parades made up of the voluntary groups and services of thanksgiving in the churches. On Saturday 12th May, formations of aircraft from the U.S.A.F. flew low over the houses. Street parties were organised for the children, with everyone contributing from their precious stocks, providing iced cakes, pastries, sandwiches, sweets and lemonade for everyone. Bonfires were kept going by children stripping bomb sites for anything that would burn and many an effigy of Hitler and Mussolini went up in flames.

Some people were calmer, remembering there was still a hard fight ahead to defeat Japan but the dropping of two atomic bombs hastened the end. V-E. Day was declared on the 15th August, which brought renewed celebrations, Churchill declaring, "This is your victory". With peace declared, the signs of war began to disappear. At the tube stations, the blast and light trap walls, which had made such a tortuous path, were removed, the first to go being at Tooting Broadway. Street shelters were to follow shortly. Blackout material and sticky tape were removed from windows in homes and on public transport, with street lighting being returned to normal.

The Parliamentary Elections took place on the 5th July 1945. The campaigning was vigorous and on the eve of the poll, Winston Churchill visited much of South London. He was met on East Hill by the Conservative candidate and then continued through the High Street, down Garratt Lane, to Tooting Broadway. It was not purely a political gathering as everyone turned out to cheer and the Prime Minister was visibly moved by his tumultuous reception. Subsequently, it was seen that they were thanking the man and the wartime leader of his country and not as the leader of the Conservative Party.

On election day, there was an exceptionally high turn out, 80% in Putney, which had five candidates and 89% in Wandsworth, which had three. During the war, people had become more aware of themselves and wanted a better world. The army had fostered an interest in social and political questions. However, the results of the election still came as a shock, with such a large swing to the Labour Party. Only Putney and Streatham remained under a Tory M.P., but Battersea South, Clapham, Balham and Tooting were gained by Labour, who also held Wandsworth and Battersea North.

The official peace celebrations did not take place until 1946 but the residents of the western part of Wandsworth did not have to wait so long. An invitation was sent to every householder in Putney, Roehampton and Southfields to attend a garden party to be held on the 19th and 20th September 1945, in the grounds of "Ravenswood", on West Hill, the home of Alderman Heath and the neighbouring house, "Gordondene".

Only limited council funds were available but, due to the generosity of local firms and national companies, amusements, entertainments, marquees and free teas for 11,000 children were made available. Volunteers helped prepare the gardens, erect the side shows and supervise the thousands of visitors. Despite some rain showers, everyone seems to have had a good time.

The war had changed many people's outlook on life. Women had become more independent and class barriers had been breached. People believed that the old regime had ended and that there was a new start, with great hopes for the future. They had fought and defeated the enemy together, so surely a small step towards Utopia was not impossible. Unfortunately, this did not reflect Britain's position in the post-war world. The U.S.A. had taken over as the political giant and Britain was virtually bankrupt after five years of war. There were to be many years of austerity ahead. Already in 1945, there was a shortage of food world-wide. In Britain there was less meat available than in 1944, although this was balanced by larger supplies of fish The bacon ration was reduced to 3oz and lard to 1oz per person, per week. In September, the clothing coupons were reduced to 36 a year. Rationing was to continue until July 1954.

The most noticeable effects of the war were the bombed sited and the damaged houses, which the local and county councils immediately set to work to repalce, a job that was still contining over twenty years later. However, the most lasting memory, according to many people, was not of unrellieved gloom but of community spirit and what nice, kind, friendly people we all were. The people of Battersea and Wandsworth could proudly say, "We served".

VICTORY PARTY, ASCALON STREET, BATTERSEA

WE SERVED – WARTIME ORGANISATIONS

Many of the war-time organisations have already been mentioned in the text. The following is a review of these and other groups not previously mentioned. All played their part in winning the war.

CIVIL DEFENCE FORCE

This was run by a committee headed by the Mayor, with the operational control under the Town Clerk. From the main control centre, directives were sent out, with the Medical Officer of Health in charge of casualties and medical services. Other officials included the Chief Warden, the Borough Engineer and an officer of the District Surveyor.

Administrative areas were based on the Parliamentary Divisions, divided into district and warden posts, each of the latter supervising approximately 2,750 residents. Each post was equipped with a telephone, gas, electric light, water and all necessary amenities. There was always someone on duty and often they became the first place of call for those needing help.

The local warden was usually the first person on the scene of any incident and one of the team was designated as the Incident Officer. He directed all the proceedings, sending for the appropriate rescue teams and services and reporting his activities to headquarters. On one hectic night in the blitz, the Wandsworth Civil Defence dealt with 297 bombing incidents, involving 3,000 messages over a twelve hour period.

CASUALTY SERVICES

A number of volunteers, known as Stretcher Parties, received training in early 1939. At first their number increased but, due to the rising costs, their numbers were cut. In 1943, they were renamed the Light Rescue Service, carrying out rescue work that only needed pick and shovel. They gave first aid to casualties and, during less hectic times, loaded and unloaded casualty trains, cleared unexploded incendiaries, salvaged furniture and assisted in distributing emergency coal supplies.

The Heavy Rescue Units were equipped in dealing with the mounds of rubble, locating survivors, giving first aid and helping victims to First Aid Posts. Most men were "stood down" in December 1944, leaving a skeleton service to carry on to the end of the war.

NATIONAL AND AUXILIARY FIRE SERVICES

Before the war, each city and town had its own fire brigade and it became essential to arrange for closer co-operation, co-ordination and greater mobility between the different areas. In London, there were 2,000 professional firemen and in 1938, recruiting was started for an auxiliary service. There was opposition from the regulars, who feared for their jobs, with the recruiting of women causing an even greater outcry.

When war was declared, the auxiliaries reported to their stations, clutching knife, fork and spoon, were equipped and sent to the sub-stations, which were usually at recently evacuated schools. Life soon became one long round of filling sandbags. During the 'Phony War', many of the recruits were thought of as "war-dodgers and parasites". By June 1940, the Government had to stop the resignations due to this pressure, as numbers were falling dangerously low.

With the threat of invasion, the personnel mounted guard at the stations usually armed only with sticks or anything else they could lay their

AUXILIARY FIRE SERVICE AT HOTHAM ROAD PUTNEY

hands on. The real test came during the 'Blitz' and the local teams were soon involved, not only locally but all over London and even further afield. The women recruits worked as telephonists, canteen staff or drove converted taxis, which towed the trailer pumps. These grey, utilitarian objects soon became automatically associated with the fire service.

The firemen became the heroes of the hour. Many were killed or injured doing their duty. Although tired, dirty and hungry, they were always ready to man the pumps and not once did they fail.

THE HOME GUARD

The story of the Home Guard is well known. Nearly 20,000 men made up the local battalions and their duties included the guarding of important factories, bridges and other vital points, manning road blocks and assisting the police during air raids. Later in the war, they even operated anti-aircraft artillery. The local battalions were: 13th County of London (Clapham); 27th C. of L. (Roehampton); 29th C. of L. (Battersea); 30th C. of L. (Tooting); 31st C. of L. (Streatham); 52nd C. of L. (Wand-Gas) and 56th C. of L. (Balham). There were also units formed by London Transport and many of the larger companies.

By the autumn of 1944, the Home Guard was told to "stand easy". The battalions were then gradually disbanded, with the local units holding their final parades in November 1944, their task done.

THE TERRITORIAL ARMY

During 1939, the various units were brought to readiness and making sure their numbers were up to strength. Each month, a quarter of the men from each company were sent to camp for war basic-training. The units included anti-aircraft companies, infantry and armoured companies. At the outbreak of war, they were quickly incorporated into the full time forces.

CADET CORPS AND OTHER GROUPS

AIR TRAINING CORPS

These were originally known as the Air Defence Cadet Squadrons and were formed to provide partly trained personnel for the R.A.F. In Wandsworth, the 34F Balham and Tooting Squadron was officially recognised in January 1939.

It was based at Fircroft Road School, Tooting and had a compliment of 60 cadets.

The aim was to have a cadet squadron in each of the parliamentary divisions and in July, 1939, the 34F and the newly formed 82nd Wandsworth squadrons paraded in King George's Park to receive their new colours. Further units were raised in Battersea, Putney, Clapham and Streatham. After war had been declared, the organisation was officially recognised by the Air Ministry and the lads were eager to rush off to help the R.A.F. In February 1941, the name was changed to the Air Training Corp, each squadron membership having risen to around 200. Over 2,000 passed into the R.A.F. from the local units, already having a good basic knowledge of airmanship and engineering. Womens Junior Air Corps Formed in 1941 along similar lines to the A.T.C. The girls, less fortunate than the boys, had to pay for their own uniforms and band instruments. There were at least three companies and some women went on to join the Forces or to essential war work.

GIRLS TRAINING CORPS

Established in Wandsworth in January 1942, its object was to provide general training for National Service, munitions work or the land army. Each parliamentary division had its own company, recruiting girls between the ages of 14 and 19. Training was given in first aid, fire-fighting, despatch carrying, drill and P.T. There were also lessons in motor mechanics, morse and secretarial duties. Much of their time was used in staffing canteens for the other cadet forces and raising money for the war effort. However, it was not all work, as instruction was given in ballroom dancing and social evenings were a regular event.

ARMY AND SEA CADETS

Both were started in early 1942, with the army units coming under the supervision of the 5th County of London Cadet Battalion. A unit at Streatham was attached to a searchlight regiment, while at Battersea, the cadets were associated with an armoured vehicles regiment. Both organisations have continued since the war.

SCOUTS AND GUIDES

While not war-time organisations, they did fine work, although the evacuation depleted their numbers. The Scouts, amongst other activities, erected many Morrison shelters and some earned a War Service badge for salvage and messenger work. The Guides raised considerable sums of money not only for the war effort but for relief work abroad.

WOMENS VOLUNTARY SERVICE

Started in 1938, this organisation was like no other in the world. The founder and chairman, Lady Reading, came to speak at Wandsworth Town Hall in May 1940, to explain about the organisation and to appeal for recruits. The aim was to supply the human, friendly and neighbourly touch in difficult times. As the organisation grew, additional centres were created at Coventry Hall, Streatham, Putney High Street and, later in 1941, at Upper Tooting Road through the efforts of Councillor Mrs Goodrich. There were 80 different jobs that the 4,000 members could do, including serving tea, making bandages and pyjamas for hospitals, knitting for the services, helping with the evacuation, driving all sorts of transport and providing emergency clothing.

The main task at the end of 1940 was the organisation of Rest Centres, of which there were 24 in Wandsworth and others in Battersea, mainly in church halls. They also handled clothing needs, distributing donations from home and abroad. Evacuated children were sent shoes and clothing, some of which were purchased using the Lord Mayor's Fund. For those rehoused, the W.V.S. went along to help with the cleaning and putting up of 'black-out' material. They were also very active in collecting salvage and savings during the national appeals.

Whatever the circumstances, the W.V.S. were always quickly on the scene, whether serving tea and snacks, giving comfort to air raid victims and helping them to places of shelter.

AMBULANCE AND FIRST AID SERVICES

The full time ambulance service was administered by the London County Council but was controlled by the Metropolitan Boroughs. They also trained the volunteers of the Auxiliary Ambulance Service, which was formed in 1938. At the outbreak of war, the auxiliaries, mainly women, reported 'to their ambulance stations. They found these had little furniture and the 'ambulances' turned out to be anything from a converted 'Greenline' bus to a local firm's delivery van. Gradually the service became fully equipped and the grey-painted vehicles, with their four stretcher racks, became familiar sights.

There were eight first aid posts in Wandsworth, with another in Battersea. A Light and Heavy Moblie Unit was attached to each post, which enabled prompt action to be taken to rescue and minister to the injured.

RED CROSS CADETS
CHEERFUL CASUALTY

ST JOHN'S AMBULANCE BRIGADE AND THE RED CROSS

Even before the war, members of the St. John's Ambulance Brigade undertook such duties as fitting gas masks and running classes in first aid. When the war started, the Medical Officers rapidly accepted their help. Both organisations were part of stretcher parties as well as staffing first aid posts and helping in hospitals.

The Red Cross also had offices where relatives of prisoners-of-war or those missing in action could go for help and advice. Welfare workers also visited all service patients and air raid casualties in hospital at least twice a week.

PENNY-A-WEEK RED CROSS FUND

This was run jointly by the two organisations and helped by other organisations, who made weekly, house-to-house collections. During the war years, nearly £100,000 was collected locally to pay for first-aid medical supplies.

THE POLICE

War saw the proliferation of new regulations, all of which had to be supervised by the police with tact. Many an argument arose over black-out regulations. The job was more difficult because of lack of staff. Some of the gap was filled by recalling recently retired men and enlisting war-time Special Constables.

As well as fighting crime, the police had the additional task of trying to control the black-market and searching for deserters and absentees from the Forces. The streets still had to be patrolled day and night, raids or no raids. Often it was the man on the beat, himself shaken by blast, who was first on the scene, searching for people trapped in the rubble. Afterwards came the dreary, tedious hours of rerouting traffic and guarding the remains of homes from looters and morbid sightseers. Many of the "men in blue" won bravery awards for risking their own lives during rescue work.

CITIZENS ADVICE BUREAUX AND INFORMATION CENTRES

The C.A.B. service was opened in Wandsworth on the 4th September 1939 at the Town Hall, under the auspices of the Family Welfare Association. The original purpose was to advise on all matters connected with the war but more and more people asked about income tax, old age pensions, housing and personal difficulties. Additional branches had to be opened due to the increase of enquiries during the war years.

By November 1940, the Wandsworth Town Hall became an information centre for most of the statutory and voluntary organisations. After heavy air-raids, temporary centres were often set up near the worst incidents. In one year alone, nearly 20,000 enquiries were dealt with by the centres.

THE LORD MAYOR'S NATIONAL AIR RAID DISTRESS FUND

This was started in 1940 to assist those who had suffered in any way through enemy action. The fund was administered by local councillors who gave grants for clothing, household effects, bedding, furniture removals, funeral expenses, re-establishment of small businesses and cash grants for immediate needs.

NATIONAL SAVINGS MOVEMENT

The movement was zealously supported in the two boroughs by a vast army of voluntary workers, under control and divisional committees. The street collectors operated in all weathers, making regular house visits. There were also special weeks of intensive effort under such designations as "War Weapons", "Warships", "Salute the Soldier", "Wings for Victory", "Thanksgiving" and "Silver Lining Campaign". The staggering total of over £30 million was collected, two-thirds of which comprised small savings.

LIGHT RESCUE VAN, KING GEORGE'S PARK, WANDSWORTH

INDEX

FACTS AND FIGURES

Number of bombs dropped on	Battersea	Wandsworth
High Explosives, mines, etc.	629	2,100
Incendaries, Oil Bombs, A.A. shells	10,000 approx.	40,000
V-1s or flying bombs	36	124
V-2s or rockets	1	7
Domestic property in 1939	28,500	76,000
Destroyed or demolished	2,515	4,157
Badly damaged	1,897	14,575
Lesser damage	24,046	53,969
Total	28,468	72,701
Civilian casualties killed	513	1,301
Seriously injured	No figures	2,191
Slightly injured	"	4,205
Population in 1939	141,700	340,000
Population in 1945	85,380	251,510

FURTHER READING

CALDER, Angus — The People's war: Britain 1939-45. *Cape 1969*

GRANT, Ian & MADDREN — The City at war. *Jupiter Books. 1975*

GRAVES, Charles — London Transport at war. *L.T. 1978*

LONGMATE, Norman — The Doddlebugs: the story of the flying bomb *Hutchinson. 1981*

LONGMATE, Norman — The Home Front: an anthology, 1938-45. *Chatto and Windus. 1981*

LONGMATE, Norman — How we lived then: a history of everyday life during the Second World War. *Hutchinson. 1971*

MACK, Joanna & HUMPHRIES, Steve — London at war. *Sidgewick & J. 1985*

MORGAN'S AT WAR — a story of achievement under fire, 1939-45. *Morgan Crucible Co. Ltd. 1946*

PEACE CELEBRATIONS — of Putney, Roehampton and Southfields... *Wandsworth Borough Council. 1946*

PERRY, Colin — Boy in the Blitz. *The Author. 1980.*